JAPAN HOUSES

IDEAS FOR 21ST CENTURY LIVING

by Marcia Iwatate and Geeta K. Mehta

photographs by Nacása & Partners Inc

TUTTLE Publishing

Tokyo | Rutland, Vermont | Singapore

Contents

New Japan House in the 21st Century

by Geeta K. Mehta

The Japanese house provides a valuable paradigm in the search for new directions in residential architecture in the 21st century. Japan is a wealthy nation of innovative people and highly developed architectural traditions. The outstanding features of Japanese design at its best continue to be the same as they have been throughout history; contemporary materials now give the design a new vigor, rendered with a characteristic Japanese panache. A sense of flowing space, integration of the interior with the exterior, materiality that expresses the essence of each material, and a strong tradition of exquisite craftsmanship—these timeless principles come alive again in the new Japanese house.

In some ways, the contemporary architects whose work is featured in this book work in an environment relatively free of the technical and economic constraints present almost everywhere else. Considerations such as a structure's longevity and its size and comfort—the main design criteria in most other countries—are not high priorities in Japan. The constraints on Japanese design arise primarily from the scarcity of land and the small sized residential lots typical of this heavily populated island nation. The homes in this book have managed to overcome the challenge presented by limited space, either because they are located outside crowded cities, or because of the design strategies that eliminate the visual clutter of the surroundings to create havens that are serene and inspiring.

Many of these homes are vacation homes built in settings of great natural beauty. They are noteworthy for the innovative ways in which they open to nature, building on traditional elements and techniques. In addition to windows, they feature entire walls that slide away to open the room to the outdoors. Inside, the rooms themselves often open one into another, blurring the demarcation between spaces, both interior and exterior, and inviting the landscape and seasons to flow in. This merger is

in part accomplished through the use of extending the floor and ceiling materials from the interior to the exterior of the house. Doorframes and sliding rails are embedded into the floor and ceilings to guide the eye effortlessly from the interior to the exterior. This is how the Zig House & Zag House (page 32) and I House (page 142) invite their lush surroundings in. On the other hand, the tiny Engawa House (page 52) uses these same techniques to successfully expand its sense of space.

A flowing sense of space, even when the area is small, is also enhanced by the creation of uninterrupted surfaces in soft natural colors that expand the line of sight, instead of drawing the eye inwards, towards objects such as windows, artwork, fussy moldings or hardware. Traditional Japanese craftsmen excelled at simplifying details, and exaggerating a few selected joints or details for aesthetic effect. These same principles are now being applied to new materials such as textured or tinted concrete, large tempered glass surfaces, fiberglass and fiber-reinforced plastics. Materiality is a forte of Japanese architecture. The time-honored high standard of workmanship that is still available today, albeit at a price, has been coupled with exciting new materials, resulting in a recognizable style that is Contemporary Japanese. Most homes in this book were designed by relatively young architects willing to experiment with materials and detailing that, though new, underscore traditional concepts. The poured concrete floors of the Karuizawa Gallery Villa (page 148), the dark stained concrete exterior of the Roundscape House (page 112) are good examples of this.

Things usually taken for granted in a private home, such as the functionality of the kitchen and bathroom, are challenged and reinvented in several houses in this book, with privacy often given a lower priority, as in the Karuizawa Gallery Villa (page 148). Unlike in the West, privacy and comfort in Japan are negoti-

able in the quest for an aesthetic living environment. This may in part be because over time the Japanese have developed social mores that allow individuals relative privacy even in public spaces. The same considerations allow for personal privacy even when the living room, bedrooms, and other areas in a Japanese home flow into each other, as in the Engawa House (page 52) and Roundscape House (page 112). Space constraints are further reflected in the small or open kitchens common in contemporary Japanese homes. Many houses, including some of the luxurious ones in this book, only have one bathroom to serve the whole family. Indeed, having any bath in a house is a luxury that became common only in recent decades. Long after World War II, public baths (*sento*) have continued to fulfil this need in certain areas.

In Japan, where even the largest and most richly detailed building is worth only a fraction of the land on which it stands, structures are torn down and re-erected with relative abandon. An average building lasts only 20–30 years, serving only one-third of its potential useful life. Historically, such frequent rebuilding was necessary to replace wood that had rotted in the country's high humidity, or had burned in frequent fires. The current frenzy for re-construction is, however, driven by Japanese construction companies that often deliberately build obsolescence into their structures and count on repeat business from loyal clients. The recent throw-away architectural culture is a regrettable development in a country where traditional homes were 100% natural, sustainable, and recyclable. Evolving earthquake laws are often used to justify the *tatekae*, or the rebuilding process now. The construction industry accounts for a whopping 12-14 percent of Japan's GNP, compared with an average of 6 percent in other developed countries.

Japanese homes are small, partly due to successive subdivisions of land in residential areas as a result of high inheritance taxes.

Inheritors usually have to sell part of their land to pay so-called "death duties," as Japan's socialistic tax regime envisages the liquidation of all large land assets in about three generations. The result in most Japanese cities is a mosaic of small, densely packed lots. Cramming all the necessary spaces of a home into a small lot, while at the same time evoking nature and creating a feeling of spaciousness, is a huge challenge, one which is well met in several houses in this book, including the Aobadai House (page 94), the M House (page 118) and Kunitachi House (page 130). "Less can be more" in the hands of Japanese architects. While few people can afford a large house, many middle-income people do invest in vacation homes away from the cities to create their dream living environments.

In most homes today, traditional Japanese elements and *tatami* rooms are conspicuous by their absence. Traditional homes in Japan, as elsewhere, are losing popularity as people choose dwellings that are more comfortable, easier to maintain, and support modern conveniences like central heating and air conditioning. In Fukuoka, Arata Isozaki invited several well-known international architects in 1991 to design the best in public housing in a project called Nexus. While some architects incorporated traditional Japanese elements into their designs, most did not. The houses most in demand were those without *tatami* mat rooms and other Japanese elements. Yet the homes in this book use traditional Japanese elements in some form in a thoroughly modern way with great success. Examples of this are the *shoji* paper screens in IS House (page 18) and the façade and *tatami* room of the Koyama residence (Page 100).

Many houses featured in this book have special spaces reminiscent of the timelessness found in traditional Japanese homes. The hearth in Nojiriko Villa (page 46) and the pitched ceilings in M House (page 118) achieve this almost effortlessly. What is

absent in a Japanese home is just as important as what is there. Elimination of the inessential has always been an intrinsic part of Japanese architecture. This sensibility still exists in many of the homes presented in this book, alongside the fashionable kitchen systems imported from Italy.

The allegiance to the masters of classical modern design is strong as seen in the Abstract House (page 26) and in many other homes in this book. The modern aesthetic is so close to the spirit of Japanese architecture that this fondness is not surprising. The slogans of Modernism, such as "form follows function" and "less is more," could well have originated in Japan, and were probably influenced by it via architects such as Bruno Taut and Frank Lloyd Wright, who were ardent students of Japanese architecture.

It is also important to put the beautiful houses in this book in the broader context of contemporary Japanese housing. Most Japanese do not live in houses of this quality. Over 35 percent of the population lives in small mid-rise apartments within large projects called *danchi*, built by the Housing and Urban Development Corporation (HUDCO). Founded after World War II to shelter the thousands left homeless after the firebombs of 1945, HUDCO started with the ambitious goal of providing one-room units for all families. People ate, slept, and sometimes even cooked in these spaces. Bathrooms and community spaces were shared. Critics who called these spaces "rabbit hutches" missed the point that these small dwellings were complemented by increasingly superb social services, such as education, health care, and law enforcement. Housing projects similar in size and design to the low income public housing that prompted riots in the United States are considered middle-class housing in Japan, and have spawned a highly motivated and disciplined workforce that has turned Japan

into an economic superpower. The ability of people to live well in small homes is determined by the quality of the surrounding public spaces, and the municipal and commercial services. Such elements and facilities are extremely well managed in Japanese cities. The luxurious homes shown in this book do not feature large garages, basements full of storage, and multiple refrigerators, as their space programs are informed by the public amenities around them, often just a short walk down a pedestrian friendly street.

Contemporary homes and lifestyles in Japan and elsewhere continue to evolve as science and technology advance. Le Corbusier, the founding father of Modernism, once claimed: "If we eliminate from our hearts and minds all dead concepts in regard to houses and look at the question from a critical and objective point of view, we shall arrive at the House Machine." The houses in this book are *not* machines: they are poetry and sculpture. The N Guesthouse (page 76), I House (page 142), and Kiyosato Gallery (page 166) are soaring in their sculpturesque ambitions. In the 21st century, with machines available for everything else, the house does not need to be a machine, but rather a base from which to deal with the rest of the world and its changes. The quintessential Japanese house has always been that. Comfort is often sacrificed for poetry. Everything that can be eliminated is, and the calm space that is achieved is enhanced with a few symbols to evoke nature and beauty. Residential spaces conducive to contemplation, and nurturing of things sacred in life, like the traditional tea huts of Japan, are needed today more than ever before. Homes today must balance our rush for things bigger and better, our efforts to live effortless lives, and the stress we put on becoming stress free. The homes presented in this book are examples of that.

Kashima Surf Villa

Architect Manabu Chiba, Manabu Chiba Architects
Location Kashima City, Ibaraki Prefecture
Floor Area 195.76 m² **Completion** 2003

Kashima Surf Villa sits right on the edge of the ocean in Ibaraki Prefecture. Although vacation cooperatives and time-share arrangements are common in resort areas in other countries, until very recently they were rare in Japan, largely because of legal restrictions on the ownership of joint property. The idea for this cooperative grew out of the many conversations the architect had with the people he met on his surfing trips to the area. The cooperative arrangement enables young surfers to own vacation property that is more intensively utilized than normal vacation homes and is therefore less wasteful in economic as well as environmental terms. The villa is meant to be fully used by the owners and their friends, all bound together by a common love of surfing.

From the outset, the architect rejected the idea of the conventional plan for inns, which has rooms arrayed along corridors. Based upon his childhood memories of shared and private spaces, he has been working toward creating "white spaces," called *yohaku* in Japanese, that are not meant for a preconceived purpose, but for chance encounters and spontaneous use. Although such spaces exist in museums and cafés, the architect feels they are also relevant to private and semi-private homes. In this project, the *yohaku* forms the communal core for nine private bedrooms and a sleeping loft, all skillfully arranged to accommodate up to eighteen people at a time. The total floor area of the villa is 200 square meters. Two bathrooms, one for men and another for women, are located so that people can shower upon returning from surfing trips. The ownership of the cooperative, as well as the management, has been kept flexible, in keeping with the lifestyle of the surfers.

Left: Luxury in this simple steel-frame wood-clad villa is defined not in terms of large private bedrooms with attached bathrooms, but rather as a place to hang out with a community of people with a shared passion for surfing. The concept for the villa evolved over dinners after various surfing expeditions, at which the merits of having individual condominium-style rooms versus shared common spaces were discussed. Because the cooperative arrangement and the details of the villa were thoroughly agreed with the clients from the start, no changes were necessary to the design once it had been finalized.

Above: Two staircases, part of a system of large sculptural block-like volumes that jut out into the double-height communal spaces, both define the spaces and inject drama. The staircases are also an important part of the steel-frame structure, holding up the upper-level bedrooms that appear to be suspended from the ceiling. The two living and dining spaces, one seen at right and the other below the staircase on the left, have been located diagonally across from each other, visually connected through the sculpted volumes, and creating a spacious feeling in what is a relatively small villa. Since children and the elderly are not expected to use the villa, the railings are also sculpturesque and minimal. Light and shadows form as much a part of the space as the furnishings.

Above and left: Kashima Surf Villa, situated along an exposed beach, is a steel-framed building clad in wood. Choosing the exterior finish for a structure in this location was a challenge because of the prevailing humidity and sea air. The architect decided on wood in consultation with his clients, who agreed to have the exterior washed frequently to minimize damage from the salt air. Large doors and windows in the living/dining areas open to spectacular ocean views and breezes, while small ribbon windows provide light to the bedrooms. The double-height space shown on the left is one of the two communal "white spaces" in the villa: "white" here refers not to the color, but to the fact that the spaces can be used according to fancy. The architect designed the 3.6-meter-long dining table and chairs. All interior surfaces, except for the floor, are painted white.

Left: Each of the four high-ceiling bedrooms is fitted with three bunk beds. Ladders provide access to the upper bunks. No storage space is provided in the bedrooms or elsewhere in the house as cooperative members do not own a particular room. Most arrive in their SUVs, which act as their storage space on these trips.

Left: The double-height space is what the architect calls *yohaku*. Surfers place their equipment on the cement floor before they wash and go to their rooms. The sharp lines of the staircase above form a dynamic pattern, along with the sunlight and shadows.

Below: The kitchen on the first floor is visible from the approach to the bedrooms on the second floor. Two staircases on the left (not shown) lead to the four bedrooms on the third floor.

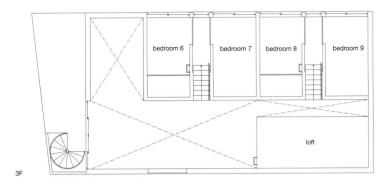

3F

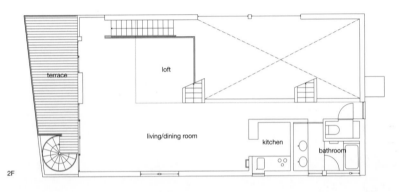

2F

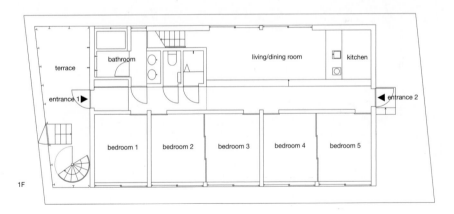

1F

N

IS House

Architect Makoto Shin Watanabe & Yoko Kinoshita, ADH Architects
Location Sapporo City, Hokkaido
Floor Area 202.66 m² **Completion** 2003

IS House was designed for a couple, both practicing physicians, and their two small children. The brief to the architects was for a house which allowed busy family members to have maximum interaction with each other. This was a perfect commission for ADH Architects, who have been developing the concept of CPS (Common spaces; Path or transient spaces; Satellites or private spaces) to address the changing needs of families in Japan, especially families in which the mother works outside the home. The result is an open-plan home with pivotal common spaces and private satellite spaces.

On the ground floor, the living, dining, and kitchen areas flow into the sunroom, while on the second floor all the bedrooms have been planned around a family room with removable walls to provide visual connectivity. The walls can be closed at night, a feature adopted from traditional Japanese architecture. A grandmother, who lives next door, helps out with many of the household chores, and her needs were also taken into consideration when locating the living, dining, and kitchen areas on the ground floor.

The architects have developed a successful strategy for dealing with the severe winters in Hokkaido, the northern-most island of Japan. The house has been divided into two zones. A double-height sunroom is located on the perimeter to the south, while utility areas such as the entrance, storage, closets, and library are located to the north. These spaces, where people do not need to spend long periods, were conceived as a buffer zone. The living room, dining room, bedrooms, and family room form the inner zone and are concentrated in the center, insulated by the surrounding buffer zone. As a result of this insulating strategy, combined with effective use of sunshine captured through massive blinds on the southern side, the house does not require heating during the day in the winter months.

Although constructed with modern technology and materials, the house also draws on Japan's rich architectural traditions. The *engawa*-like sunroom and *sudare*-like louvers that cover the entire front façade are among the concepts that have been given a new interpretation in this house.

Opposite and above: Giant anodized aluminum blinds, manufactured by Hunter Douglas, cover the entire front of the house and serve a dual function. The angle of the blinds has been positioned so that in summer they protect the interior from direct sunshine, while in winter they absorb solar heat. They also provide privacy in the crowded residential area of Sapporo; although passers-by cannot look inside the house, the occupants can see out. While these blinds would have delighted Le Corbusier, the legendary guru of *brise soleil*, their expansive use to cover an entire façade is a reference to *sudare*, traditional Japanese bamboo blinds.

Left, below and right: The double-height sunroom is akin to the *engawa*—an intermediary space between the outside and the inside—of Sukiya-style traditional Japanese homes. When the sliding glass windows are opened, the space becomes part of the garden, and when they are closed, it serves to expand the interior. The living and dining rooms, located on the ground floor, can thus be completely opened to the garden. The shadows from the louvers form an ever-changing pattern on the walls. A freestanding platform comprises the first step of the staircase located in the center of the house. This platform is reminiscent of a *tobi ishi*, a large stone placed outside traditional Japanese teahouses, for guests to step on to before climbing through the small crawl door into the tea-house. Three bridges made of metal grating along the top of the sunroom form small balconies for the bedrooms located on the second floor.

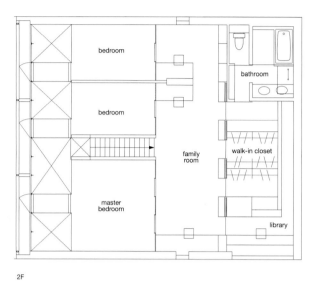

2F

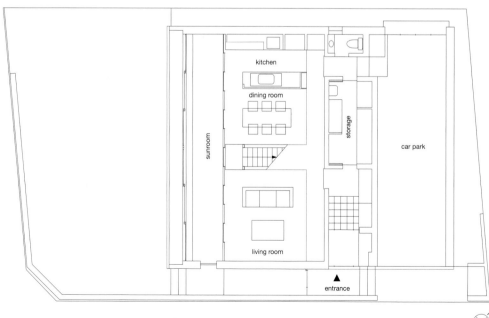

1F

Opposite top left: The ladder in the bathroom leads to the roof tower for when snow-related maintenance is necessary, but also doubles as a towel rack. The exit hatch at the top of the ladder also serves as a skylight.

Opposite: The floors of the three bedrooms shown in the plans have been raised three steps above the level of the floor of the family room to provide a skip space for light to enter.

Above: The furniture in the family room has been built in to provide an uninterrupted open space for the children to run around. The desk at the far end of the room is at the same level as the bedroom floors. The steps leading to the bedrooms have storage shelves and drawers built into them. Designed like caddies, they can be pulled up to the desk when needed. The design of the steps is an innovative interpretation of another traditional Japanese element, the *kaidan dansu* or step chest.

Opposite: In the bedrooms, entire walls made of *fusuma*-like sliding doors can be opened during the day for better interaction among family members. The walls can be readily closed at night for privacy, as is the custom in traditional Japanese homes

Left: The window treatment in the bedrooms has been specially designed for this house by ADH Architects, and is an innovative interpretation of the traditional *shoji* screen. Vertically folding screens made of Japanese handmade *washi* paper are faced with acrylic to render them stain-and-tear resistant, and then mounted on wooden frames.

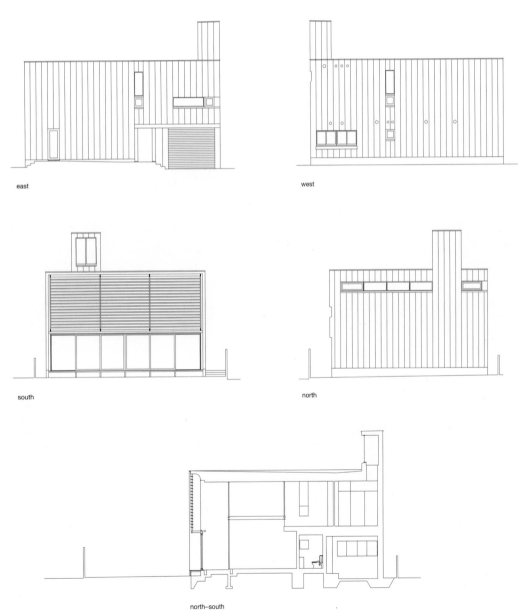

east

west

south

north

north–south

Abstract House

Architect Shinichi Ogawa, Shinichi Ogawa & Associates
Location Onomichi City, Hiroshima Prefecture
Floor Area 89.68 m² **Completion** 2002

The High Modernist style in architecture and furniture design never fails to delight and influence both producers and consumers of design. The owner of Abstract House enjoys collecting classic mid-20th century furniture, while the architect cites Mies Van der Rohe, the guru of Modernism, as his main inspiration. The owner and the architect instinctively understood each other's design aspirations in the initial discussions on Abstract House, a situation highly conducive to an outstanding result.

The house has a surprisingly simple plan. It is basically a rectangular white box, with two long sides comprising solid concrete walls and two shorter ends made of frosted glass. A flat roof slab forms a neat top to the box. Another small and narrow rectangular box, measuring 2.4 meters x 9 meters x 1.8 meters, has been placed in the center of the larger box. This smaller box, which accommodates the bathroom, walk-in closet, and other storage space, has been conceived as a piece of furniture rather than merely as another room. Because all ancillary spaces and storage shelves have been neatly arranged in this second, smaller box, the remaining areas in the house are completely open and flexible. The open space to the west of the smaller box accommodates the kitchen, dining, and living rooms, while the open space on the eastern side is used as a bedroom. The size and quality of the interior spaces was the primary focus of the design, rather than the exterior design, which simply resembles a stark white box. The amused owner has reported occasional confusion by people coming to deliver mail or packages.

Small courtyards have been laid at the north and south ends of the house. Tall boundary walls made of frosted glass provide privacy to the courtyards, a major requirement in the high-density residential neighborhood in which the house is located. These courtyards are extensions of the rooms, their doors sliding open to bring in light, wind, and the seasonal colors of the foliage. The marble flooring in the rooms, heated from below during the winter, has been extended at the same level to enhance the feeling of the courtyard being an integral part of the living space.

Previous spread: Abstract House glows at night from light issuing through the frosted glass wall enclosing the front courtyard.

Above: The sliding doors to the living room and bedroom can be opened to the front courtyard, increasing the amount of living space and bringing the outside in. The open-plan kitchen at the far end of the living room opens out to the rear courtyard. The level and material of the flooring in the interior extend out to the courtyards, reinforcing the sense of continuity. The smaller rectangular box visible in the center of the larger box accommodates the bathroom and storage functions of the house. The entrance area is defined by a two-paneled *byobu* screen. The coffee table and lamp in the living room were designed by master sculptor Isamu Noguchi.

Opposite bottom: The kitchen, seen from the rear courtyard adjoining it, continues the theme of stark simplicity. Against the all-white back-ground of the house, the owners have stamped their personality with their choice of furniture, their pottery collection, and other decorative accents.

Above: A sensual view of the living room and front courtyard in the evening light. The concrete side walls of the courtyard can be used as a screen for projecting views of nature—a virtual abstract garden—family photographs, or even movies. Spotlights enhance the trees planted against the frosted glass front wall. The two molded plywood chairs in the living room were designed by Charles and Ray Eames in 1946, and were named the best design of the century by *Time Magazine* in 2000. The red one was a present from the owner to his wife, who enjoys moving it to different locations, using it as a red accent against the largely white house.

west

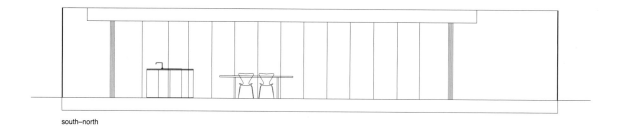

south–north

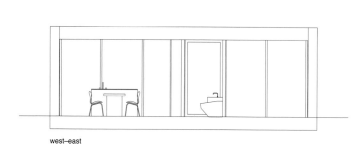

west–east

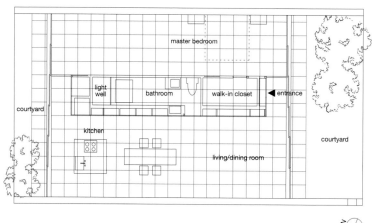

Opposite: In keeping with the highest principles of Modernism, every little detail in the house has been meticulously designed so that it becomes fully integrated into the surfaces of structural elements such as walls and floors. These hidden details allow the space in the house to become the main focus. The plan, elevation, and section drawings of the house reveal a masterful design in which all mechanical elements and construction details are hidden.

Above: The bedroom looks out on to the front courtyard and the frosted glass boundary wall.

Right: The glass wall of the bathroom contributes to the overall feeling of spaciousness and light that is an intrinsic feature of the house.

Zig House & Zag House

Architect Nobuaki Furuya, NASCA

Location Setagaya-ku, Tokyo

Floor Area 359.86 m² **Completion** 2001

Right: Viewed from the central courtyard of the house, a covered terrace forms the entrance to both wings of the house: the architect's on the right and his parents' on the left. The living rooms of the two wings adjoin the terrace, allowing easy access between the wings and providing a larger area for family gatherings.

Below: Two types of façade face the courtyard. The walls of the architect's living room on the far side of the courtyard consist of 75-mm-thick composite board segments alternating with windows, while those on the side of the parents' living room are completely glazed from the floor to the ceiling of the second floor.

Architects often test the limits of their design philosophies when they build houses for themselves. The Zig House & Zag House, located in a residential section of Setagaya district in Tokyo, is one such example. Influenced in his student days by the work of the famous master J. Hejduk, Nobuaki Furuya believes that houses should be perceived as but one layer along a continuum of enclosures for human beings, starting from clothes and moving on to outer environments, such as house, garden, city, and space beyond. He maintains that these layers should be as flexible as possible, allowing for changes in the size, structure, and lifestyle of families. This has been the basic concept underlying several houses he has designed since 1990.

Built for three generations of a family living together, the house comprises two independent units—Zig and Zag—connected by a double-height covered terrace. The architect, his wife, two children, and a parrot occupy one wing (Zag), while the other wing (Zig) has been planned for the architect's parents. All areas have been designed as simple connectable box-like spaces, allowing for maximum flexibility. The main rooms in the architect's wing are separated by partitions which can be readily moved to form one large, spacious area. The architect also paid special attention to the site, saving most of the trees and designing the house around them. This resulted in the zigzag shape of the house, reflected in its name.

The house is constructed of a system of simple frames that have been placed on an 1800-mm grid. These composite assemblies are made from pressure-bonded Japanese cypress wood manufactured in the Okutama area of Tokyo. The main areas of the house are arranged inside these frames on two levels. In addition to the movable partitions, storage furniture such as cabinets and kitchen units have also been designed to be movable, adding to the overall flexibility of usage.

Left and right: The structural system of the house comprises simple frames made of pressure-bonded wood placed on an 1800-mm grid, with all other elements of the house fitting neatly into this vertical and horizontal system. The beams of the frames are 130 x 380 mm thick and the columns 130 x 130 mm. The height of the ceiling of the parents' living room (foreground) is lower than in the architect's wing, in keeping with the aesthetic requirements of the *tatami* matted room situated on the ground floor behind the living room.

Below: All hints of the usual window-sill or parapet have been removed in the floor-to-ceiling windows facing the inner courtyard, invoking a treehouse-like feeling. This has been achieved through meticulous detailing of the window frames. The floors on the second floor are made of 60-mm-thick composite Japanese cedar wood, which complements beautifully the exposed wood of the supporting structure.

Above: Floor-to-ceiling windows in the architect's living room help to bring the beauty of the outdoors in, and contribute to the feeling of openness characteristic of the entire house.

Left: The unique circular stone bath is carved out of a single piece of stone. The bathroom in which it is located is a roofed, lean-to structure attached to the back of the main house. Storage and other ancillary functions are also accommodated in this peripheral structure, a solution common in traditional Japanese homes.

east–west

Right: In the dining area in the parents' part of the house, autumn leaves reflected in the glass table echo the glory of autumn colors in the courtyard.

Below: The plans and elevation show the organization of various spaces in the house. The structure and foundations are made of thick planks of composite wood designed to resist earthquakes and fires. Radiant air conditioning and heating fixtures have been integrated into the ceilings. The hot water supply system incorporates an eco-friendly aero-thermal mechanism that uses carbon dioxide as a cooling medium.

Shizuoka G House

Architect Chiharu Sugi & Manami Takahashi, Plannet Works
Location Shizuoka City, Shizuoka Prefecture
Floor Area 700.97 m² **Completion** 2003

Below: The large double-height windows of the second-and third-floor living areas of the house can be shaded by closing the fiber-reinforced plastic (FRP) perforated sliding screens located on the outer edge of the balcony. The FRP screen is reminiscent of the *sudare* bamboo blinds of traditional Japanese homes that were hung in summer to provide shade, privacy, and a cool ambience, while still allowing the occupants a view of the outdoors. The balcony itself is a contemporary rendition of the traditional *engawa*, a transitional space that could be used as part of the outdoors or indoors, depending on which side of it was opened. The large curved window on the top floor is part of the master bedroom suite.

Right: The dining room on the second floor looks towards the sitting area. The dining table and chairs were imported from the Italian company Storato. Behind the sofa is a *tatami* mat room with a wooden ceiling that contrasts with the rest of the contemporary materials used in this room.

Shizuoka G House is situated along beautiful Suruga Bay in Shizuoka Prefecture. The steep drop from the shore to the water makes the sea dangerous for swimming, but also produces the serene atmosphere that enticed the owner, a long-time resident of Shizuoka, to choose this place for his new house. The site was also selected in response to the wishes of his mother who wanted to live in a house with a view of both the sea and Mount Fuji.

The architects and the client agreed that the ocean should not simply form a view from the house, but should shape the life within it. The plan of the house is thus organized into three horizontal zones parallel to the sea. The first floor is primarily devoted to a work-cum-meeting room and a storage room for the owner's books. The second floor, which includes a spacious dining room, living room, *tatami* mat room, and kitchen, is the entertainment hub. The third floor has a bedroom suite for the owner's mother, while the top floor contains the master bedroom suite, a spare bedroom, and a sitting area. Since the site is on a slope and the ground floor of the house is lower than the highway it faces (Route 150), the living areas have been located on the upper floors to take advantage of the great views above the level of the highway.

Entertaining is a very important part of the owner's life-style, and therefore the architects were asked to design a kitchen to include heavy-duty professional-grade equipment not usually found in private homes. Most of the kitchen equipment, as well as the kitchen and dining room furniture, was imported from overseas, based on the architects' digital designs e-mailed to the manufacturer.

Because of the stringent aseismic building regulations applying to this part of Japan, the structure of the first three floors comprises thick concrete walls and roller-compacted concrete (RCC) columns. Since the fourth floor has many partition walls that act as stiffeners, a light steel structure has been employed here. The architects believe that the exterior of a house should be designed to last, while the interior should be flexible enough to accommodate the changing needs of its occupants. With this in mind, they designed the house to be as open and flexible as possible. Instead of including additional textures or finishes, plain, unadorned architectural materials have been allowed to define the character of the interior.

Above: The main entrance to the house is graced with a door made from beautifully grained reddish-brown chestnut wood. The door helps to soften the impact of the "hard" materials used here and inside the relatively cavernous entrance hall (left).

Left: The exposed concrete of the walls and ceiling, and the 300 x 300-mm Italian porcelain tiles on the floor. The narrow stairwell from the entrance sets the stage for the surprisingly expansive living and dining areas on the second floor, which are flooded with light and offer wonderful ocean views through the mostly open south face of the house. The display alcove in the entrance hall is surrounded by cabinets for storing shoes, a response to the traditional Japanese custom of changing footwear from shoes to slippers upon entering a house.

Right: The landing of the staircase leading up from the ground floor to the second floor is covered with the same porcelain tiles. The walls here, as in most other parts of the house, have been made of exposed concrete with a wax finish. The wooden ceiling on the *tatami* mat room can be seen through the glass on the right. Natural light enters this space from the unusual placement of openings at the top and bottom of the walls, while leaving the middle of the walls in intentional twilight.

Right: The walls of the client's work and meeting room on the ground floor are made of exposed concrete with square formwork. The large showcase on the right as well as the table in the center have been custom-assembled with aluminum-molded parts made by Ecomsfit. They were specially made to display the owner's Peanuts cartoon character collection, which includes vintage as well as rare token pieces. The Aeron chair is by Herman Miller. The floor lamp has been assembled from parts normally used for street lighting on expressways.

Below: The house elevations highlight the simplicity of the design, details of which are carried through to the boundary walls.

Opposite: The expansive quality of space achieved on the second floor is apparent in this view from the back of the dining room looking out toward the ocean.

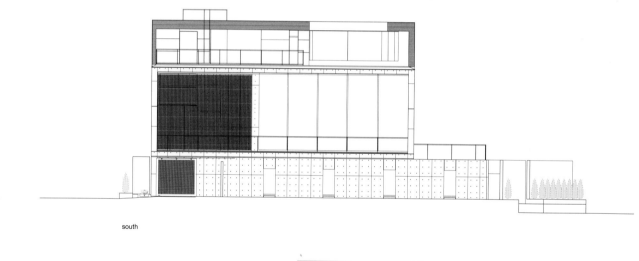

south

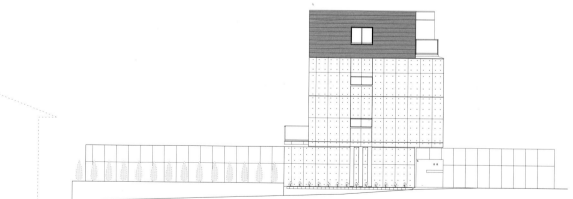

west

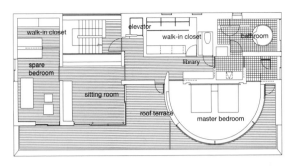

4F

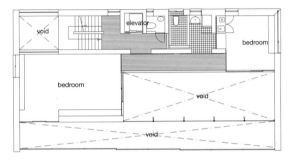

3F

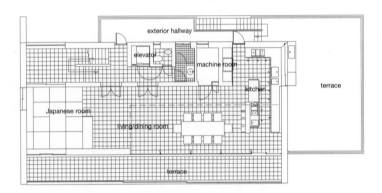

2F

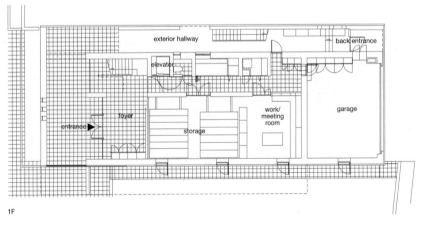

1F

Above: The FRP perforated screen on the *engawa*-style balcony in front of the living area has been drawn to provide shade and privacy to this area. This screen material was selected for its effectiveness in weathering sea air.

Left: The kitchen island immediately behind the dining table on the second floor serves as a bar or snack nook. It contains a built-in gas oven and double ceramic cooking range, as well as a "performance" barbeque grill, small sink, refrigerator, and freezer. The L-shaped area at the rear of the kitchen houses the more heavy-duty professional-grade equipment. A section of the kitchen not visible to guests accommodates the "tall unit zone," where full-height cabinets provide plenty of shelf space for equipment and food storage. All kitchen counters are 80 cm high to accommodate the imported dish-washer and other appliances. The chestnut wood kitchen cabinetry and the sculptur-esque table top, as well as the dining table, chairs, and stools are from the well-known Italian company Storato. The pendant lights, called Popone, were designed by Pepe Tanzi. The space from the kitch-en flows to the third floor corridor via the double-height ceiling.

Right: The house plans show the clear organization of space into work areas on the ground floor, living and entertainment areas on the second floor, and private areas on the third and fourth floors.

Nojiriko Villa

Architect Masashi Yagi & Konomi Yagi, Yagi Architectural Design
Location Shinano Town, Nagano Prefecture
Floor Area 86.14 m² **Completion** 2003

The owner of the Nojiriko Villa is a cooking teacher, who commissioned the architects to design a house in which she could enjoy nature away from the hustle and bustle of Tokyo where she mostly works. Primarily a place of rest, the house was also intended to serve as a cooking studio where she could demonstrate her culinary art using fresh local ingredients of the sort not easily available in big cities. For this reason, the owner specified that a long cooking counter be the centerpiece of her house. She also asked that the entire place be utterly simple, that only black and white be used, and that the end product be a place that would make everything and everybody appear beautiful.

The architects greeted these ideas, which were close to their own hearts, with enthusiasm. After taking into consideration the client's personality and requests, as well as the site conditions, they arrived at a simple plan enclosed within two non-concentric arcs. Taking advantage of what they thought was the greatest asset of the site—the forest surrounding it—they opened the entire west wall to the views. The topography and the views demanded that a large part of the house jut out over the steep site, supported by a wooden framework. Softer land in the area meant that the structural loads had to be carefully distributed. Local wood, as opposed to imported wood, was used for both the exterior and interior of the house. The architects believe that Japan's recent dependence on imported wood has resulted in the near extinction of the domestic timber industry and in the neglect of its timber forests. As moisture and condensation are a problem in vacation homes in this area, the interior walls have been finished with painted mud plaster that is effective in dehumidifying the house during the damp summer months.

The Nojiriko Villa expresses the philosophy of both the client and the architects, who believe that the beauty of a structure should not come from conscious effort but from an honest response to a commission, a site, and environmental conditions. Using rigorous discipline, anything that was not essential in the house has been eliminated, resulting in a Zen-like composition in black and white.

Opposite and above: Nojiriko Villa juts out dramatically over a steep, tree-clothed drop. The exterior of the house as well as the supporting framework have been constructed of locally grown timber. The architects made minimal change to the landform of the site, preserving as many trees as possible.

Above: The dining area looks out to the narrow deck which runs the length of the building, and toward the wonderful forest view. Columns have been set back from the glass curtain wall. The floor is made from locally grown larch wood (*karamatsu*).

Below: A storage space for logs is built under the section of the counter that functions as a fireplace or coffee table.

Right: The dining, kitchen, and living areas fill one large, high-ceilinged space. The sizable chimney acts as an exhaust for cooking smells as well as smoke from the fireplace. The multi-purpose counter was specially designed: ventilation has been provided between the wood base below and the counter top, which is made of layers of sheetrock, silica calcium board, and polyethylene film, finished with white concrete. The whole area opens to great views to the west. A narrow band of windows along the top of the eastern face allows for additional light and cross-ventilation in summer.

Left: A continuous glass wall opens the house to views and sunlight from the west.

Right: The strict color scheme of black and white has been carried through to the owner's uncluttered bedroom. The beam is part of a system of exposed framework in the house.

Below: The plan of the house shows its simple organization within two non-concentric arcs. The entrance door leads to a smartly stark space that sets the tone and color scheme of the house. This space also serves to insulate the kitchen and living areas from the cold wind. The elevation and section drawings show the spectacular way in which the house is perched on a steep mountain site. The roof has been steeply pitched to deal with over two meters of snow that fall in this area every winter.

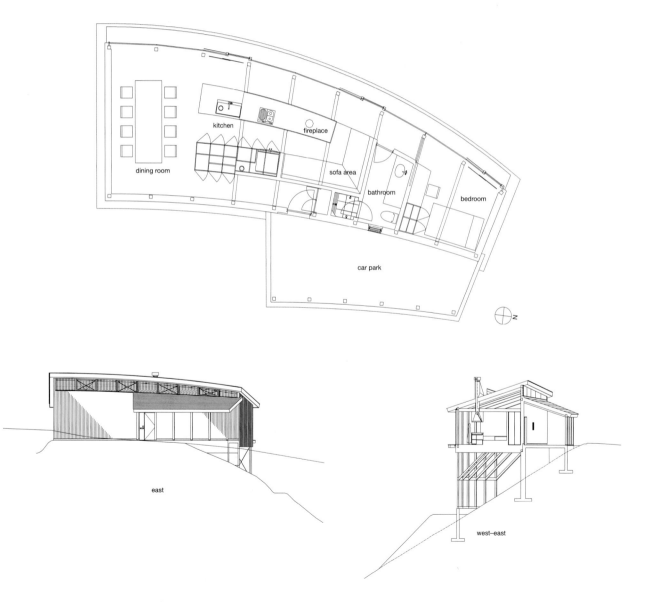

kitchen

fireplace

dining room

sofa area

bathroom

bedroom

car park

N

east

west–east

Engawa House

Architect Takaharu Tezuka & Yui Tezuka, Tezuka
  Architects, Masahiro Ikeda, Masahiro Ikeda Co., Ltd.
Location Setagaya-ku, Tokyo
Floor Area 78.48 m² **Completion** 2003

An *engawa* is a long, narrow space, somewhat like a
verandah or patio, with sliding screens, often included
in traditional Japanese architecture. Engawa House was
given its name during the garden party held to celebrate
its completion, when its sliding doors were opened to
the garden and guests declared that the house resem-
bled an *engawa*. The nine sliding glass doors facing the
interior of the Engawa House can be pulled across to
provide privacy or opened to allow access to the *engawa*
or garden. Sliding storm shutters on the garden side
provide an extra layer of protection during winter. The
engawa thus serves as a place from which to enjoy the
garden as well as additional floor space for the house.
Engawa House sits on a narrow lot sandwiched between
the home of the wife's parents on the north, and a street
on the south. The wife and her husband were delighted
to find the lot on the other side of this wall, and decided
to build a house close to their extended family.

   Planning the house was an exercise in thinking "within the box." The spatial needs of the couple and their
two children have been fitted into a simple rectangle 16.2
meters long and 4.6 meters wide. A 2.2-meter-high wall
on the street side gives privacy to the house, while a continuous strip of sliding windows above this wall provides
a view of the sky and allows sunlight to enter. The opposite wall, on the north, consists of sliding glass doors.

   The interior of the house was conceived as a single
harmonious space. All partition walls have been limited
to a height of 2.1 meters. Since the roof height is 3.5
meters, there is uninterrupted space above the partitions, adding to the feeling of spaciousness and facilitat-
ing ventilation.

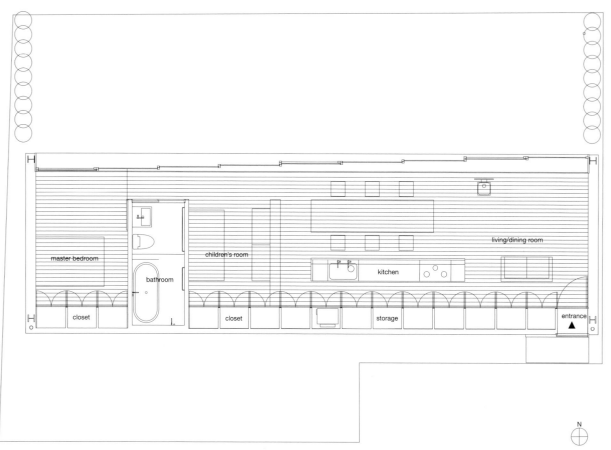

master bedroom

bathroom

children's room

living/dining room

closet

closet

kitchen

storage

entrance

N

Left top: The narrow box that defines Engawa House has a refreshing simplicity. The kitchen and dining area are separated by a low stainless steel partition. Instead of the usual hood and exhaust fans, effective in removing only about 70 percent of kitchen fumes, the tall ceiling allows any smoke to drift upwards, from where it disperses through the high windows. The difference in height between the northern and southern openings creates a natural airflow that facilitates this process. The low height of the single-story house helps sunshine reach the garden. In summer, hot air rises toward the roof, and naturally exits through the high windows. Steam rising from the bathtub provides humidity to counter Japan's dry winter weather. The pedestal-type fireplace, a trademark of the architects' residential designs, has been placed between the living and dining areas to serve both. The grooves on the floor for the sliding glass are a common feature in traditional Japanese architecture.

Right, top and bottom: The partitions between the various living spaces in the house rise from the floor to a height of only 2.1 meters, as in the children's bedroom, bathroom, and master bedroom shown here. In a small house like this, there was a choice between having closed-in spaces for different functions or allowing a feeling of spaciousness. The owners chose the latter. Lack of personal privacy in this arrangement is not unlike that found in traditional Japanese homes made of slender wooden elements and paper screens. The owners believe that this relative lack of privacy is a positive attribute that makes family members more considerate of each other.

Left bottom and below: The plan and section show the bold simplicity with which the areas of the house have been arranged. The entire south-facing wall has storage cabinets up to 2.1 meters in height. The wooden flooring and structural elements in the house, like the sliding doors facing the garden to the north, have strong reference to traditional Japanese construction techniques. However, due to the width of the span, steel reinforcements had to be added to the beams along the length of the house, above the door and window openings.

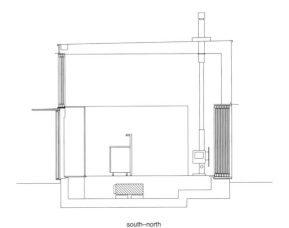

south–north

Misonou House

Architect Makoto Tanijiri, Suppose Design Office

Location Higashi Hiroshima City, Hiroshima Prefecture

Floor Area 115.29 m² **Completion** 2003

Opposite and below: The light-filled first floor of the house can be opened up like a tent by sliding away glass walls on three sides. Columns have been intentionally avoided at the corners to enhance the feeling of gravity-defying lightness. The living, dining, kitchen, and studio areas are all part of one large, airy, open space. The exterior walls of the upper floors are made of dark galvanized copper.

Located in the town of Misonou, just an hour by road from busy Hiroshima City, this house enjoys beautiful views of the rural countryside from three directions. The client, a building contractor, wanted to live with his small family as close to nature as possible. The architect responded by designing living areas that can be opened up like a tent by sliding away glass walls on three sides. Skylights complement this feeling of openness, enabling the occupants to go about their daily lives with a feeling of being outdoors. The openness of the house diminishes as one goes from the first floor to the private areas on the second floor, and from there to the loft which is lit only by a narrow ribbon window.

Opening up the ground floor on three sides gave rise to the obvious problem of temperature control. The architect

addressed this by creating a hybrid solar and mechanical heating system. The thick cement mortar floors in the living, dining, and studio areas on the ground floor act as a passive solar heating device, supplemented with a conventional hot water floor heating system. The architect believes that such hybrid systems will be necessary in order to achieve environmental sustainability in the future.

The interior organization of this 115-square meter house has been expressed externally as a composition of inter-acting sash-like surfaces and volumes without the usual heavy corner supports. The architect wanted each room to be defined by its views and light, rather than by hard geometrical forms. The cladding on the exterior is made of dark galvanized copper.

Above: The house enjoys expansive views of the agricultural countryside on three sides, an increasingly rare privilege in Japan. The great view toward the north inspired the architect to create the tent-like open spaces on the ground floor. The furnishings echo the horizontality of the house and landscape.

Left: The crisp minimalist lines of the staircase and custom-made kitchen reinforce the feeling of calm in the house. The architect wanted the views around the house, rather than strong geometric forms, to mold the spaces. Translucent polycarbonate partitions separate the living/dining room from the entrance and the client's studio.

Right top: The volume of the loft modulates the double-height space of the family room. The loft is a snug hide-away, a perfect place to tickle the imagination of a young child. It is approached by a ladder from the family room. White walls on these upper floors contribute to the feeling of lightness and provide a contrast to the dark wood flooring. The small horizontal windows frame broad views of the countryside.

Right bottom: The elevations of the house highlight the planes and block-like volumes that articulate the organization of spaces within. The window openings are largest on the ground floor, decreasing in size to mere ribbons in the family room and loft.

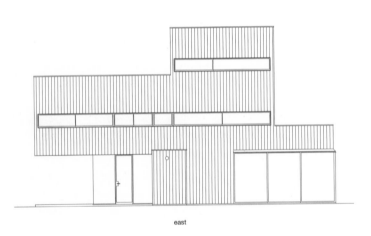
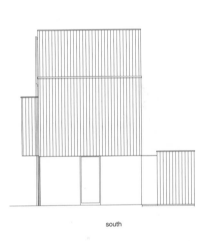

east

south

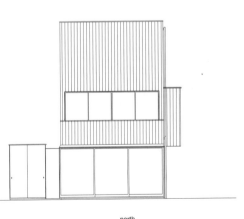

west

north

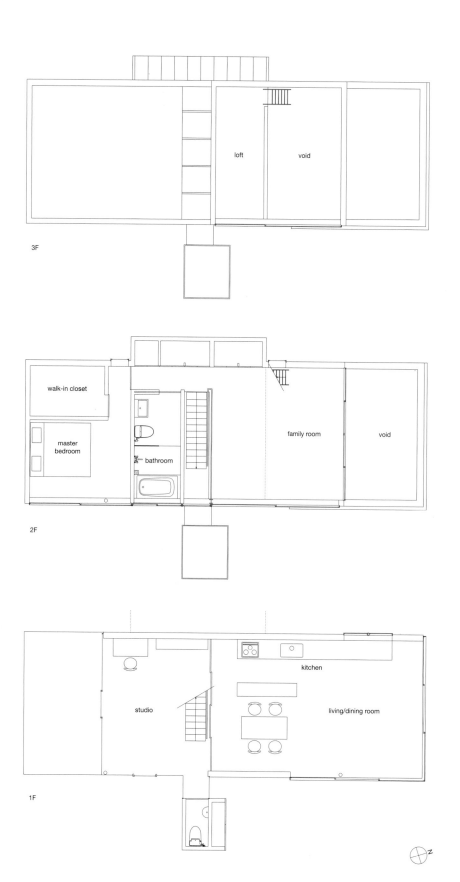

3F

loft   void

2F

walk-in closet

master
bedroom

bathroom

family room   void

1F

studio

kitchen

living/dining room

N

Left: Arrangement of the rooms has been kept simple to take advantage of the open landscape surrounding the house, as shown in the plans. The feeling of openness is reinforced by the double-height ceilings in the staircase, living room, and family room, and by the use of skylights.

Below: The guest toilet and the adjoining storage shed for gardening equipment form a free-standing structure on the first floor. The narrow toilet is made dramatic by the use of a glass skylight, an unexpected feature.

Right: The exterior walls of this part of the house are made of stainless steel. The deep second-floor overhang over the patio on the south side of the house provides shade. Columns have been avoided at the corners. A graveled area surrounding the concrete patio floor is used for parking cars.

Sukiya Extension

Architect Tomoyuki Utsumi, Milligram Studio
Location Karuizawa Town, Nagano Prefecture
Floor Area 130.15 m² **Completion** 2004

The Sukiya-style cottage at the near end of the new arc-shaped extension is a good example of a traditional Japanese building deeply influenced by the ideals of Zen Buddhism and the tea ceremony. Using humble natural materials, the style aspired to achieve the high aesthetics of simplicity and minimalism. The extension was planned with sensitivity to the 90-year-old cottage, with the façade along the inner arc being designed to echo the materials and rhythm of the posts of the old structure. The original Japanese garden situated between the cottage and the extension has also been restored.

Nestled among mountains and woods, Karuizawa resort is a popular escape a mere hour away from the summer heat of Tokyo. Almost nine decades ago, the famous statesman Okuma Shigenobu (1838–1922) owned an estate here on which stood a large three-story Western-style mansion and a small Sukiya-style cottage. While the mansion has long gone, the diminutive cottage survived several changes of ownership. Conversion to a vacation house involved repairs to the long-neglected cottage and the addition of a new living room, dining room, kitchen, and bedroom suite.

The architect translated the clients' brief into an arc-shaped extension, at one end connecting to the Sukiya-style cottage and, at the other, floating out over a steep slope. Left intact were a 3-meter-high stone wall, the garden, and a gently curving stone stairway which were all part of the original mansion. This stairway now leads to the entrance of the new wing. The addition harmonizes beautifully with the old cottage in the choice of materials, treatment of the façade, roofline, and raised plinth.

To enable year-round use of the vacation house, and to keep it free of damp when unoccupied, the architect developed a special heating and ventilation system. The windows along the southwest side were designed to let the afternoon sun into the house. When the roll blinds are closed, they cause the heat to rise up, setting convection currents in motion. When the temperature differential between the upper and lower parts of the room

Above left and right: The extension (left) was designed in the shape of an arc so as to meet and utilize the 3-meter stone wall and staircase left over from the original mansion built 90 years ago (right). The new bank of windows starts at a height corresponding to the openings of the existing cottage, but gradually increases in height as the building curves toward the wall. The double-glazed windows, with their roll blinds, are an integral part of a system designed to keep the house heated and ventilated when unoccupied. The roof ridge follows an eccentric curve, going diagonally across the arc-shaped building, but giving a thoroughly contemporary look to the end of the new wing, which floats out over a steep slope, supported by a funnel-shaped structure designed to preserve the old staircase, which now leads to the entrance of the new wing. The roof and rear walls of the extension are finished with copper plates. There are no windows on the back of the building to insure privacy from neighboring homes located nearby.

rises above a critical point, a heat sensor in the ceiling triggers a fan that circulates the heat from the upper part of the room vertically down to the flues under the floor, as well as around the room. An additional fan heater allows the house to be heated up quickly when vacationers arrive during the winter months.

This system also serves the Sukiya-style cottage with a 300 cubic-meter-per-hour fan built into the ceiling at the juncture of the old and new wing, while another fan built into the corner of the cottage draws the air out of the building. The interior of the cottage can thus be warmed without any heating system of its own.

The plan of the new wing forms an arc shape sweeping away from the old Sukiya cottage on the left. The entrance to the new wing is via the old flight of stairs on the northeast side of the house. The living, dining, and kitchen areas are located to the left of the entrance, while the bedroom and access to the cottage are located to the right.

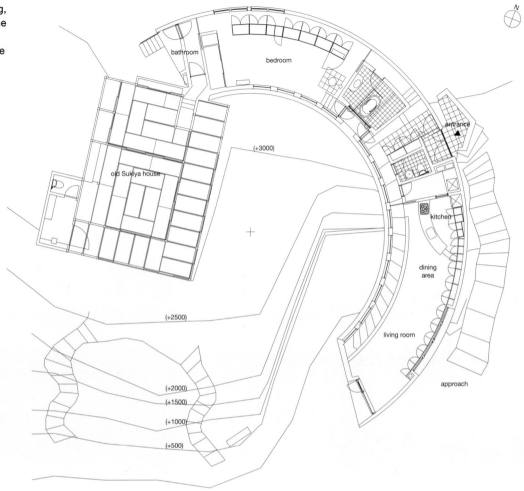

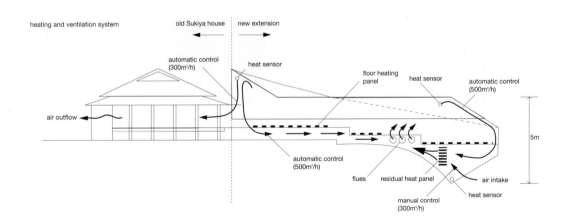

Below: An antique wood-burning fireplace gives a warm ambience to the bedroom. Placed away from the walls, the closets on the left form an independent bank.

Right: In the right half of the new arc structure, a continuous oak-floored space accommodates the living, dining, and kitchen areas. The northeastern wall is lined with cabinets while the southern wall has large glass windows that form part of the heating system. The stairs near the windows lead to an alternate entrance at the lower level for use when the main stone approach stairs are covered with ice. The chair in the foreground was designed by Mies van der Rohe in 1929 for the Barcelona Pavilion.

H House

Designer Akihito Fumita, Fumita Design Office
Site execution Miwa Kankyo
Location Shibuya-ku, Tokyo
Floor Area 193.09 m² **Completion** 2004

The H House is situated in a typical, quiet residential area in Tokyo. Part of the challenge of designing the house was to fit the various areas needed into a relatively small floor area on a small plot of land. Sunlight regulations in the Japanese Building Code, which prohibit a new structure from casting a shadow on surrounding residential properties for more than a few hours each day, were another important consideration; such regulations often result in lengthy negotiations with the municipal authorities and with neighbors. For this reason, many buildings in Japan are stepped back in height, or have slanted roofs. The dramatically cantilevered master bedroom of the H House, projecting as it does over the entrance, is a response to these restrictions, since the bedroom could not be located elsewhere in the plan.

The house has been designed as a composite of volumes and voids. Doors, window frames, ceilings, and projections have been lined up and matched as closely as possible. One example of this meticulous detailing is the ceiling of the living room which continues past the window to become the underside of the cantilever that accommodates the bedroom on the floor above. Restraint is also a feature of the color scheme and furnishings. Certain walls, cabinets, doors, and stairs have been categorized as "self-conclusive" and finished with reflective white paint, while other surfaces have been "dematerialized" with non-reflective white paint.

Every aspect of the house has been designed with the utmost care to eliminate visual clutter and to contribute to an atmosphere of balance in space. The designer believes that since the purpose of a light fixture is to provide light, it is the light that should be seen, not the fixture. With this in mind, all lighting has been built into the walls and covered with white acrylic. A similar philosophy governs the air conditioning and heating systems. Air intake and exhaust vents for the air conditioning system have been placed in slits between the walls and ceilings. Storage spaces in the house follow the same principle. Except for some visible storage along the living room wall, all other storage has been concealed behind doors.

Above: Car parking presents a design challenge, not only in the larger urban design context but also in the design of a small house. Too often garages are out of scale or are too strong-smelling to connect with the house. An innovative solution adopted here was to visually integrate the garage with the house via a glass wall. The entrance foyer is visible from the garage. The bold colors and striking shape of the Ferrari Testarossa add considerable drama to an otherwise pearly white interior. The sloping floor of the parking area is made of expanded metal while the flat area is of painted roller-compacted concrete (RCC).

Opposite: The front of the house is dominated by the cantilevered master bedroom, which springs out over the garage entrance from atop the glazed living room window. The plane of the underside of the projecting bedroom block continues inside the house to form the ceiling of the living room. This restrained play of voids and white block-like volumes defines the character of the house.

Opposite: No spectacular views surround the house. It has therefore been designed to focus inwards. A sculpturesque steel spiral staircase with glass treads, topped by a circular skylight, forms the centerpiece.

Left: The dining room and open-plan kitchen are to the left of the staircase, and the living room (above) to the right.

Above: The floor of the living room has been raised to provide sufficient height for the garage below it. The sparse furnishings and the white finishes contribute to a feeling of light and space.

Left: The square windows of the master bedroom, which looks east, are set high in the back wall. Aluminum blinds provide further privacy. The beauty of the bedroom derives from its perfect axial symmetry. All fixtures and fittings have been concealed or integrated into the infrastructure. The lighting, consisting of slim, seamless fluorescent tubes installed in rectangular indents covered with white acrylic, has been incorporated into the head-board and cupboards. The teak used for the floor-ing adds warmth to the room.

Right: The passageway leading to the bedroom has spacious closets on both sides. Ribbon win-dows above the closets let in light while aluminum louvers on the outside obstruct views of the inside.

Below: The section drawing highlights the alloca-tion of the areas in the basement and on the two floors above.

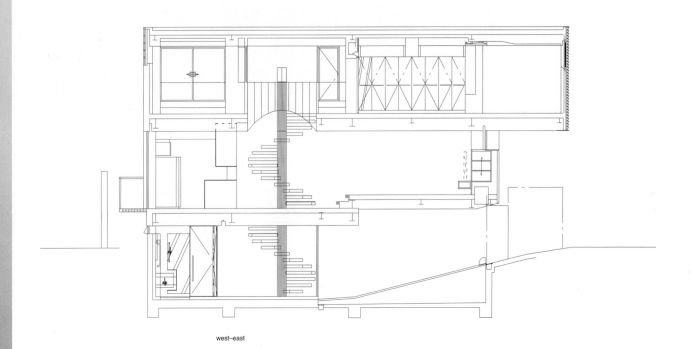

west–east

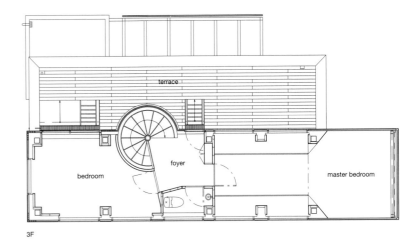

3F

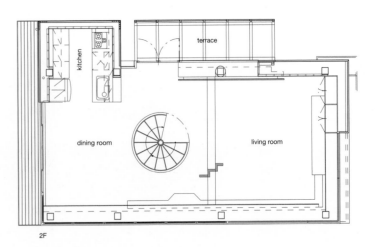

2F

Left and above: The bathroom is situated in the basement. Part of the flooring comprises teak slats, with drainage underneath, while the remaining area is covered with matte white tiles. At the far end, tall, circular storage units finished in teak veneer house towels and toiletries. A toilet (not shown) faces the cabinets. The washbasin counter extends past the glass partition into the bath/shower area at the near end. The designer's philosophy of concealing fixtures is seen in the rain shower head recessed into the ceiling.

Right: The organization of the three floors is shown in these plans.

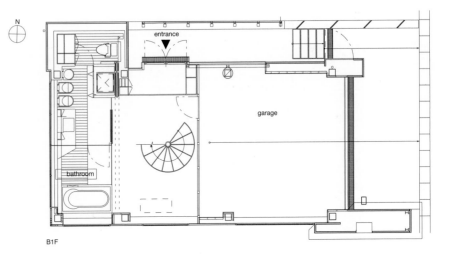

B1F

N Guesthouse

Architect Takao Shiotsuka, Takao Shiotsuka Atelier
Location S City, Oita Prefecture
Floor Area 95.90 m² **Completion** 2001

What sort of environment can best recharge tired business executives in between meetings and travel? The design of the N Guesthouse was an attempt to trigger the relaxation response via a stark but dramatic oceanfront space rather than through oversized sofas, *tatami* mats, or a more homely atmosphere. By conspicuously avoiding familiar comforts, the space seeks to transport its users toward a special state of mind, much like a Zen riddle.

All expectations, including that of a flat floor, have been challenged, indeed turned upside down, in this one-room corporate guesthouse in Oita Prefecture, Kyushu. Most of the wooden floor has been designed in the form of a staircase that starts from the rear end and descends toward the ocean. A large landing near the middle of the stairs allows up to six people to sit down for a meal, while another flat area at the bottom is a place for cooking or simply relaxing. The architect derived his inspiration from observing visitors at the owner's house relaxing and eating as they sat on the steps near the kitchen.

Unlike the typical guesthouse, this one does not provide sleeping facilities. The only piece of freestanding furniture is a simple white laminated board that forms the table on the second landing, and extends to become a kitchen counter near the window facing the ocean, further down the steps.

All visual and tactile distractions have been minimized in the guesthouse in order to draw one's attention toward the focal point: the ocean view. This view has been carefully framed by a large window. The size and proportions of the window—5 meters in height and 4 meters in width—were calculated to hide an unsightly view of adjoining factory buildings. Heat-absorbing glass has been used for the windows and this also cuts down ultraviolet rays. The view from inside the guesthouse changes dynamically as one descends the stairs. While the ocean forms the predominant view from the top of the stairs, an increasingly larger part of the sky comes into view as one goes lower. The opposite end of this tube-like interior has another large glass window that looks out toward the hilly forest at the back of the building, adding to the dramatic impact of the overall structure.

Top: A simple, rectangular, exposed concrete box, with large fixed windows at both ends, forms the exterior of the N Guesthouse, located on the edge of a bay.

Opposite and above: The owner and the architect decided on the use of exposed concrete for the exterior of the buiding in response to the rough-textured concrete of the sea wall in the area. The slope of the stepped floor inside is articulated in the bold cutout at the lower middle part of the structure.The small door and staircase along the left side serve the kitchen area.

Above: The focal point of the guesthouse is the ocean, viewed from the large window at the front. The owner, who has lived near the sea all his life, believes that the sensory elements of the open ocean can be overpowering and are therefore best seen in a more soothing atmosphere from inside a building. The result is the fixed glass window at the front that filters out the sounds of the ocean, thereby heightening the visual impact. The two large windows on either end necessitate round-the-clock air conditioning.

Right: The floor, made entirely of Laotian pine planks, is designed as a cascade of steps interspersed with three landings. The first landing is at the top of the staircase leading up to the second floor. This landing has been extended to become the top of a sideboard along the wall behind the kitchen counter. The second landing forms the dining area, while the third adjoins the window fronting the ocean. A simple white laminated board—the only piece of freestanding furniture in the guesthouse—serves two main functions: as a table on the second landing, where up to six people can be seated on large floor cushions called *zabuton*, and as a kitchen counter or bar on the third landing, where it is at a height suitable for cooking. The stove and oven are housed in an enclosed area under the exhaust hood.

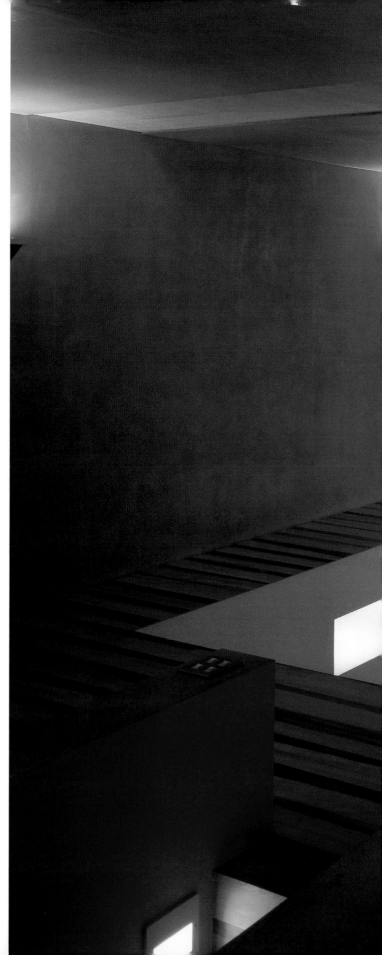

Above: The large window at the back of the upper level, shown in the south elevation drawing (right), looks out on to a forested hill. The north elevation drawing shows the large window overlooking the ocean at the front. Rendered in dramatic red, the staircase in the middle leads down to the entrance on the lower floor.

Left: From the top of the staircase, the stepped wooden floor descends to the dining area on the second landing. The first floor (not shown) houses an oval-shaped *ofuro*, the popular communal bath found in Japanese spas, and an attached open terrace with a view of the forest behind the guesthouse, shown in the lower-level plans on the right. The walls and the ceiling of the guesthouse have been finished with glossy paint to reflect the changing light on the ocean waves outside. The lighting consists of a simple rectangular recessed fixture aligned in the direction of the wooden steps, and sconce fittings along the walls.

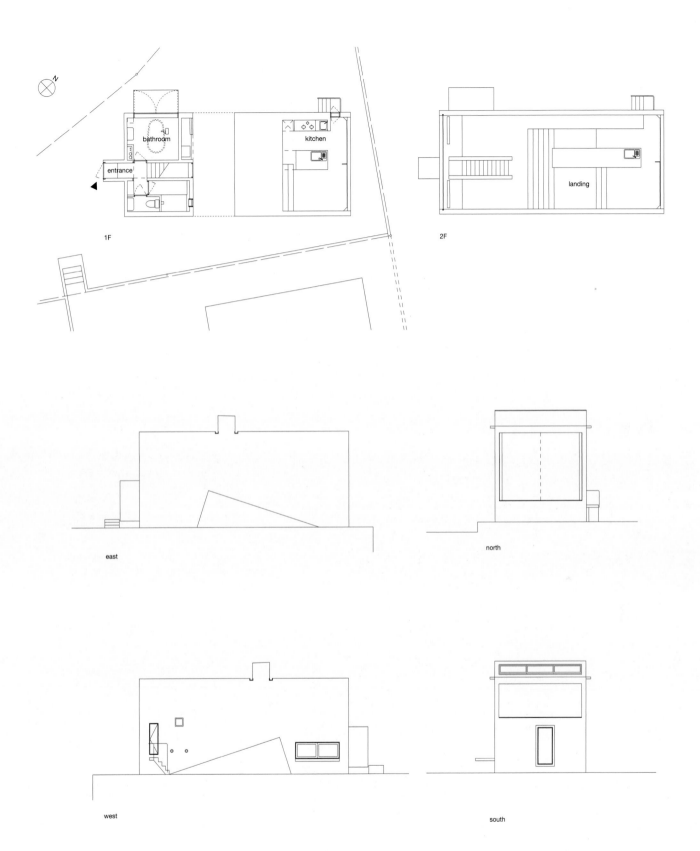

1F

entrance

bathroom

kitchen

2F

landing

east

north

west

south

Yufuin Residence

Architect Shigemi Imoto, Imoto Architects
Location Yufuin Town, Oita Prefecture
Floor Area 173.77 m² **Completion** 2004

The Yufuin Residence is located in the resort area of Oita Prefecture, famous for its beautiful views of tree-covered mountains and its natural hot springs. Exhibiting great sensitivity to the natural environment, the architect has gone to great lengths to insure that the house does not block the view of the mountains from the street by building a stepped structure into the sloping site, with the master bedroom and bathroom on the ground floor, the living, dining, and family rooms and the kitchen on the second floor, and a guest bedroom on the third level. One of the requirements of the clients was that every room in the house must have a view. The architect has fulfilled this need, and in addition has created a terrace and a courtyard that also provide great views, yet afford privacy to the occupants.

A major innovation of the house lies in the treatment of its exposed concrete walls. Although reinforced cement concrete has been hailed as the magic material of artistic freedom since the beginning of the 20th century, it has the disadvantage of creating an impersonal and cold look, compared with the warmth and handcrafted feel of wooden structures. The Yufuin Residence is one of several new structures that have been built worldwide, more particularly in Japan, that provide a solution to this problem. Formwork for the concrete used in the house was made of Japanese cedar wood (*sugi*) planks arranged in such a way that the concrete was imprinted with the pattern of the planks as well as the subtle grain of the wood. This recent refinement in material technology makes it possible to create a concrete surface with both a look and feel reminiscent of the Arts and Crafts movement. Different planes of the concrete texture of the house are highlighted as the sun moves across the sky, and as time and the elements age the material. The textured concrete walls have been carried through to the interior of the house, where they are complemented by natural materials such as bamboo and wood.

Opposite: This cozy but modern home is nestled at three levels into the slope of a hill. Heavy projecting cornices reinforce the horizontality of the house, which is made of reinforced concrete imprinted with a pattern made from Japanese cedar (*sugi*) planks; the uneven planes of the planks create an interesting texture on the surface of the house.

Above: Entry to the house is via a glass-enclosed staircase at the cedar-clad entrance gate, the only structure visible from the street. The driveway and area beyond, which form the flat roof of the living and dining area below, are also made of exposed concrete with a *sugi* formwork pattern.

Above: The same textured concrete walls used on the exterior are carried into the living room on the second floor and other living areas. Simple black and white furnishings, accented by brightly colored carpets, complement the starkness of the walls and the timber beams on the ceiling and add warmth to the room. The dark wall at the far end forms an attractive backdrop for the narrow but dramatic staircase leading to the guest room on the third floor. Heating has been installed under the exposed mortar flooring.

Above: Sliding glass doors in the dining room and the living room at a right angle to it, located on the second floor, open out to the courtyard, which is landscaped in a geometric pattern with railroad sleepers and grass and planted in the middle with a single tree. Leading off the courtyard is a terrace covered with cedar decking on concrete. Visible from the dining room is the kitchen at the far end. The floor lamp in the dining area, called Romeo Moon F, was designed by Philippe Stark. The pendant lighting, Romeo Moon S1, comes from the same series.

Left: In the master bedroom on the first floor, the transverse exposed timber beams on the ceiling balance the strong horizontal lines of the concrete walls and the louver blinds. Against these strong directional lines, the furnishings have been kept very simple, in the signature white that permeates the whole house.

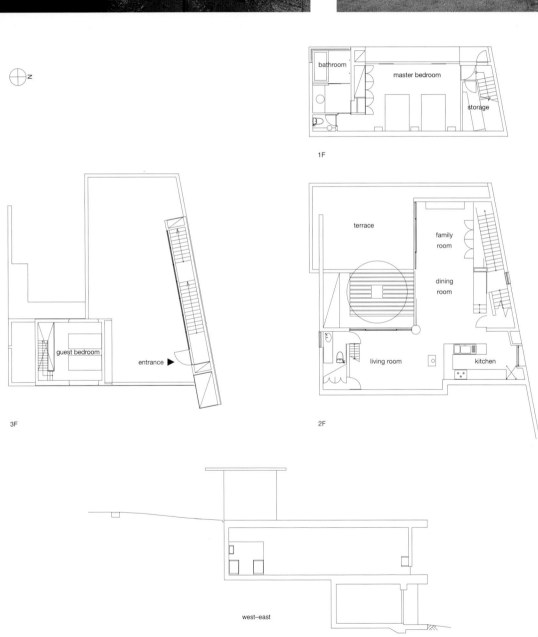

N

bathroom

master bedroom

storage

1F

guest bedroom

entrance ▶

3F

terrace

family room

dining room

living room

kitchen

2F

west–east

Opposite top left: The bathroom adjoining the master bedroom contains a tub made of Japanese cypress (*hinoki*), the preferred wood for bathtubs in Japan as its scent evokes memories of deep forests. The slate floor to the right of the tub is where one soaps and rinses one's body before stepping into the tub for a good soak. This practice not only keeps the cypress bath clean but also enables whole families to share the hot water in the tub, a tradition carried over from times when fuel for heating water was scarce in Japan. In this case, the bath is fed by a natural hot spring on the site, so needs no fuel for heating.

Opposite top right: A detached bathhouse in the garden, surrounded by Japanese oaks (*kunugi*) that were here long before the house was built, and reached by a path made of railroad sleepers, contains a *roten-buro* bath (below), also fed by the natural hot spring.

Below: *Roten-buro* baths in Japan are similar to saunas in Scandinavia, and are meant not just for bathing but for spiritual contemplation. They are carefully situated to capture the best views of the natural surroundings. The surface of the surrounding walls has been kept simple to aid the meditative quality of the space.

Katsuura Villa

Architect Manabu Chiba, Manabu Chiba Architects
Location Katsuura City, Chiba Prefecture
Floor Area 94.82 m² **Completion** 2003

Opposite: Perched atop a hill, Katsuura Villa provides a splendid view of both the woods surrounding it and the Pacific Ocean in the distance. The interior functions of this vacation home have been articulated in terms of block-like spaces fitted neatly inside a crisp cubic form.

Above: The dramatic living room window wall, uninterrupted on its two sides by any heavy frame or structural post, gives a feeling of lightness to an otherwise dark exterior. The exterior walls and the deck, which juts out over the sloping site and complements the cubic form of the house, are made of Japanese cedar (*sugi*) which has been treated with an oil-based water-repellant stain.

Katsuura Villa was designed for a couple as a tranquil retreat, a place where they could spend time with each other or simply enjoy time alone, reading a book or relaxing. Their needs were met by the concept of *hanare* (detached room), a concept which the architect has been working on for some time. The idea behind *hanare* is to create a blissful "hideout" within a house, one which is removed from the rest of the house in terms of access and appearance so that the occupants have a feeling of being away from anyone or anything. The guest bedroom on the second floor, separated from all other areas in the house and approached by a ladder, serves that purpose here.

The clients had selected a site with a good view of the Pacific Ocean for their vacation home. The architect has responded to the site and to their requirements by using a system of juxtaposed three-dimensional spaces, each with a great view of the outdoors. All interior functions, including the large garage, have been fitted neatly into a crisp cubic form. Square windows of various sizes, that also echo the form, pierce the outer cube at strategic locations. The kitchen and the double-height living space flow into each other, while the dramatic dark forms of the guest room-cum-hideout and terrace loom above. A steel truss supports the long span of the guest room projection into the living room. Clad in wood, the exterior of the house is noteworthy for its neat craftsmanship and excellent detailing.

A restrained palette has been used on the interior as well as the exterior of the house, creating harmony between them as well as with the natural environment. Japanese cedar wood (*sugi*), treated with an oil-based water-repellent stain, has been used for the exterior walls and the deck flooring. Most interior walls are finished with white paint, including the double-height living room. The flooring inside is formed of walnut parquet, making a pleasant contrast with the white walls and the dark wooden surfaces. Normally laid in a pattern such as herringbone, in this house the parquet has been made of very small pieces and installed in straight lines, giving it a mosaic-like appearance.

Left: The double-height living room forms the core of the house.

Below: Visible through the large window is the hideaway guest room and its terrace, which are reached by a wall ladder, a characteristic feature of the work of this architect (see page 15). The area behind the kitchen counter is raised by three steps from the living room floor, forming a purposely ambiguous space that also serves as the base of the staircase leading up to the master bedroom. The dark walls on the block jutting out into the living room, the dark base of the kitchen island, and the dark block shape of the kitchen chimney—all covered with an oil-stained plywood veneer finished with clear urethane—contrast with the white walls and the mosaic-like walnut parquet flooring.

Right: The stainless steel-topped kitchen island faces the large living room window and the view beyond.

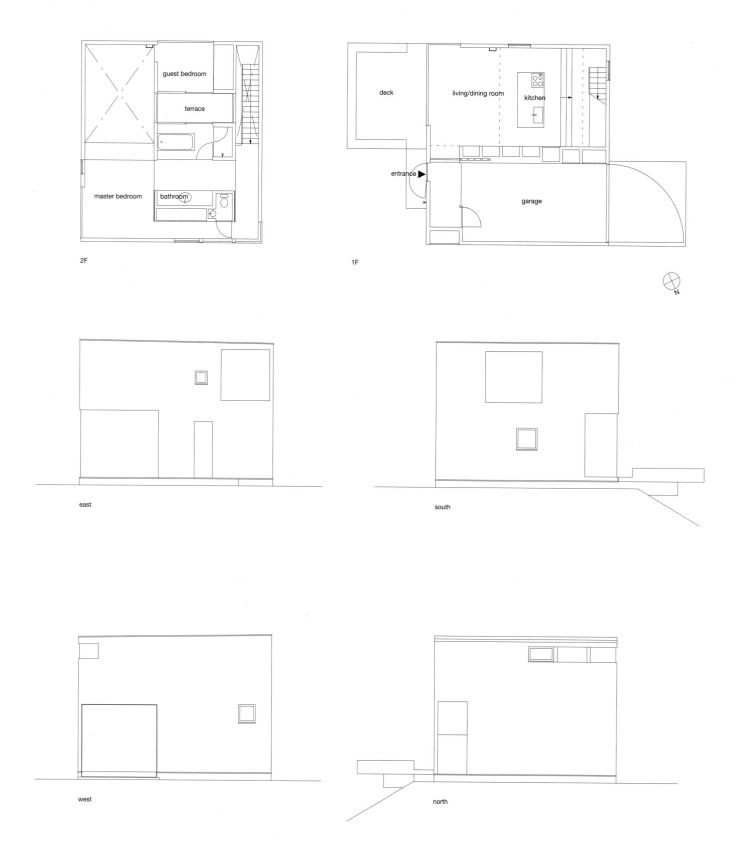

2F

1F

entrance ▶

deck

living/dining room

kitchen

garage

guest bedroom

terrace

master bedroom

bathroom

east

south

west

north

Above: The floor-to-ceiling picture window in the master bedroom has been designed to minimize the impact of the wooden frame and to maximize the view. It produces the exciting feeling of being completely open to the outside, much like being in a tree house. Together with the smaller window, which is framed with aluminum and can be opened, it echoes the square form of the house. The floor is made up of 300-mm-length walnut parquet pieces, finished with oil, another example of the superb craftsmanship employed in this house.

Right: The master bedroom on the second floor is separated from the hideaway guest room by a spacious bathroom and a terrace. The glass wall on the right looks down onto the double-height space of the living room, and through the large living room window to the landscape beyond.

Aobadai House

Architect Satoshi Okada, Satoshi Okada Architects
Location Meguro-ku, Tokyo
Floor Area 238.46 m² **Completion** 2004

This house is located in Daikanyama, one of the more fashionable areas of Tokyo. The client, a young executive, is a car aficionado. He purchased a lot in the area for his home and cars, and for entertaining friends and business clients. The four-car garage built to accommodate his car collection takes up a little over half of the long, narrow site. As the large garage had to be located on the ground floor facing the street in front, little space was available on this level for the living and dining areas. The architect's solution was to house the entrance foyer and master bedroom on this level, and to locate the living, dining, and kitchen areas, guest toilet, and two terraces on the second floor. A bold diagonal line running across the northern side of the site further divides the house into two segments. The smaller part on the north is exposed to the sky through a series of glass panels, while the larger part is covered by a single opaque roof.

The living area on the second floor is sandwiched between two terraces. The broad terrace above the garage functions as a place for entertaining guests and features a jacuzzi. A shallow water stream with a glass bottom flows along the north wall of the terrace. It acts as a skylight, letting sunlight into the garage below and casting wavering shadows on its surfaces. The rear terrace, smaller and more private, doubles up as a service area during parties. The bathroom and laundry are located on the ground floor along the southern wall, within easy reach of the garage, since the owner spends much of his spare time working on his cars.

The building laws are quite restrictive in this area, and the size and height of a building are limited by the amount of shadow that a building may cast on neighboring properties. In the case of this lot, the architectural laws and setback regulation restricted the height of the western façade to less than 5.6 meters. To design a luxurious house in this small area was a challenge that has been well met. A combination of reinforced concrete and steel has been used to make the structure of the house resistant to fires and earthquakes.

Above: The four-car garage, which takes up approximately half the area of the site, is located on the lower level at the front of the house. The high, bold wall above it insures privacy for the terrace. Exposed concrete on the walls of the ground floor contrasts with the white marble slab flooring, which is carried through from the outside walkway and gate to the front door, creating a sense of continuity.

Opposite: The concrete wall bordering the pathway cuts through the site at an angle, forming a dramatic aproach to the door. The guest toilet is located behind the translucent wall above the entrance hall.

Left: On the second floor, floor-to-ceiling double-glazed windows allow the minimum possible interruption to the flow of space from the dining and living rooms to the terrace beyond. The large window frames are custom-made of steel, painted black, while smaller window frames are formed of aluminum. The exposed concrete walls echo the exterior, at the same time providing a textual contrast to the flooring, which is made of jarrah, a water-resistant Australian hardwood. Like the marble flooring below, the wooden flooring on the second floor is continued from inside to outside without any change in level or texture to reinforce the feeling of continuity and spaciousness.

Right top: The transparent roof above the staircase leading up to the second floor is made of glass, which screens out heat and ultraviolet rays while introducing sunlight into the entrance hall on the ground level. The main entrance to the house can be glimpsed in the background. The guest toilet is at the top of the stairs.

Right bottom: The kitchen at the rear of the house is cantilevered over the staircase leading to the second floor.

Left: High concrete walls around the terrace screen it from neighboring buildings. The expansive jarrah flooring and the roof of the living and dining room, articulated on two solid concrete walls, are softened by the shallow pool on the left. Finished with marble, its green glass bottom acts as a skylight, causing waves in the water to caste a dance of shadows on the garage floor and walls below.

Opposite top: At the far end of the second-floor terrace, the jacuzzi adjoins the shallow pool running the length of the north wall.

Opposite bottom left: The bathroom of the master bedroom faces a tiny courtyard that brings in light and air.

Opposite bottom right: Located directly above the entrance, the unusually designed guest toilet is flooded with natural light coming through a translucent glass ceiling and walls.

Below: The plans below show the simple but clever organization of various parts of the house.

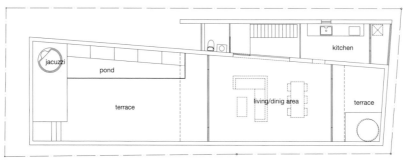

2F

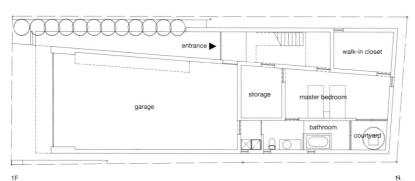

1F

Koyama Residence

Designer Hisanobu Tsujimura, Hisanobu Tsujimura Design Office
    & Moon Balance
Structural Designer Daiki Maehara / SD Room
Location Sakyo-ku, Kyoto
Floor Area 211.54 m² **Completion** 2004

Opposite: The rear of the Koyama residence evokes the timeless shape of an elemental house. The house has been constructed of reinforced concrete, and its roof and walls covered by a 25-mm-thick dark granite stone facing. Channels to catch and drain rainwater are placed at the juncture of the roof and walls. A new waterproofing material, "RC Guard," was applied to the stone facing and concrete surface. The low windows of the *tatami* room can be seen in the foreground.

Bottom: In front of the house, a tall pinewood lattice screen provides privacy.

The owners of the Koyama Residence had initially planned to remodel the old house belonging to one of their fathers into a comfortable place in which to retire, but eventually decided to build a completely new and "aggressively free" house. They wanted a place they would enjoy living in, yet one that was easy to maintain as they got older. The designer worked closely with them on these goals. He believes that the participation of owners in the evolving design of a residential project is of critical importance, unlike commercial projects that are usually only evaluated in terms of their commercial success. He likens the design process to painting a picture. He provides a fine white canvas on which the residents of the house fill in the details to reflect their lifestyle and personalities. His role is simply to set the scene, leading people to contribute their own ideas.

In the design of this house, the designer was influenced by the timeless quality of house-shaped sculptures by Katsuji Wakisaka, which resemble the drawings of houses done by young children, as well as the simple and understated lifestyle of the American Shaker sect. Traditional Japanese architecture has many things in common with the aesthetics of the Shakers, including a love of wood and simplicity.

Organic building materials such as stone, wood, and paper have been used where possible in the construction of the house in recognition of the fact that such materials become even more beautiful over time. Traditional elements such as *shoji* screens and *tatami* mats have been employed in the interior to make the house comfortable and to remind future generations of the positive traditions of family and of Japanese culture.

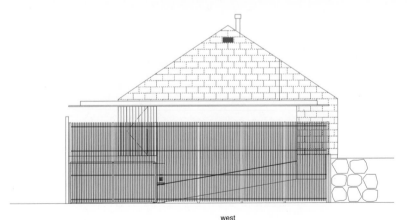

west

Opposite and above: Stone, wood, and other natural materials that age gracefully over time have been used in both the construction of the house and the furnishings. Skylights above the double-height living and dining area (opposite), which is sandwiched between the open-plan kitchen (above) and the master bedroom, flood the house with light. A pedestal-type wood-burning fire-place warms the whole house, while niches built into the wall of the living/dining area accommodate the large flat-screen television and other related equipment. *Shoji* screens can be pulled aside for a view of the courtyard and garden. The dining table and other built-in furniture are by the house's designer. Located on the second floor, beyond the glass railing, is a study and adjoining library.

Left: The elevation drawing shows the simple form of the house. The joints of the roof and walls and the peripheral screen have been meticulously detailed so as not to detract from the proportions of the main form.

Left: Ample space has been provided for books, pottery, and other objects in the study on the second floor. An adjoining library insures adequate space for books. The study is very well lit by the skylight in front of it as well as by the concealed lighting in the floor, walls, and ceiling, which can be adjusted to complement changes in the amount of light entering the skylight during the course of a day. Other fixtures and mechanical elements, such as the air conditioning, have also been hidden as far as possible. The Aeron chair is by Herman Miller. The restful white walls and the light wood floors provide an ideal backdrop for the owners to stamp their personality on the house.

Right top: The *tatami* room, cantilevered above the bedroom, is reached by a light steel staircase. Its tall ceiling and simple glass railing, which echoes that bordering the study, allow a free flow of space between the two rooms. A wooden border surrounds the Ryukyu-style square mats in the *tatami* room.

Right bottom: Lighting has been built into the bed's headboard, while the air conditioning unit has been concealed along the top of the wall behind the bed. Windows at floor level allow in more light.

Below: The plans illustrate the simple organization of the living spaces on two levels and the interplay of single-storied and double-height spaces.

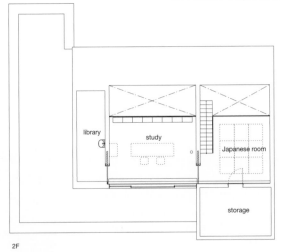

2F

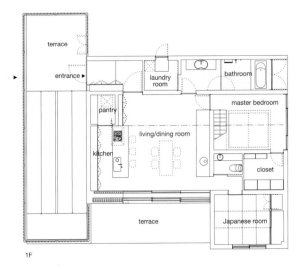

1F

O House

Architect Jun Aoki & Associates
Location Setagaya-ku, Tokyo
Floor Area 455.59 m² **Completion** 1996

Above: The playful composition of rectangular and circular shapes arranged in horizontal and vertical planes is exhibited in the façade of the second and third floors and the terrace on the second floor. The random patterned stone on the terrace, which has been laminated to blur its natural texture, continues inside the second floor, integrating the two areas. The sculpturesque steel elements on top of the roof contribute to the playful spirit of the house design.

Opposite: A circular staircase leading to the living room on the second floor mirrors the shape of the circular breakfast room on the ground floor, while a straight flight of stairs leads to the third-floor bedrooms. The solid upper parts of the living room walls cleverly block the cluttered view of the neighborhood, but slit windows placed at the bottom of the walls let in light.

The challenge in designing this house, as with many houses in Japan, was to create an oasis of calm and privacy in a high-density residential area. Trees and gardens slowly disappear in such neighborhoods as lots planned for single-family homes get subdivided into increasingly smaller lots. The architect responded to this situation by invoking a feeling of being in a garden environment through the incorporation of small, circular gardens within the living areas, thus blurring the distinction between the inside and the out.

While rejecting the contextual relationship of a crowded neighborhood, the architect, inspired by the movie "Bad Blood" by director Leos Carax, has tried to create what he calls a "zero-gravity" space that belongs "neither here nor there." The architect believes that such zero-gravity spaces can be realized by mixing reality and fiction until one is barely distinguishable from the other. In this house, the concept is manifested in such details as floors made of randomly laminated real stone to make them appear fake and, conversely, fake wood which has been made to look real.

The various spaces of the house have been organized on three floors, with each level relating to the outside in a different way. Although the first-floor kitchen, storage areas, and garage have no direct visual connection to the surroundings, the breakfast room on this level is an introverted space facing a small circular garden, while the concave study looks out to an enclosed garden. The second floor, which faces the surrounding houses, has also been designed to avoid the sight lines from neighboring houses. The only connection with the outside here is the horizontal slit window on the lower part of the living room wall that lets in sunlight without compromising privacy. Since the view is relatively open at the third floor level, a continuous band of large windows has been installed all around at floor level.

The architect likes to compare this house to a park where people—here the residents—pass each other, meet, and communicate in a playful environment. This spirit of playfulness is evident in the circular and rectangular forms that interact on horizontal and vertical planes in the house, as well as in details like the sculpturesque railing on the roof.

Left: One end of the dining room opens out to a terrace which overlooks three of the four gardens placed strategically around the house, all delightful interpretations of *naka niwa*, tiny gardens inside traditional Japanese homes designed to help bring nature into a tightly packed urban environment.

Above: The concave-shaped study on the ground floor, accessed by stairs from the living room, looks out to the largest of these gardens, a broad, semicircular garden bounded by a wall.

Right: The section drawing shows the organization of the house. The structural system varies on each level. While steel has been used for the top floor and reinforced concrete for the lowest level, steel and reinforced concrete have been combined on the second floor.

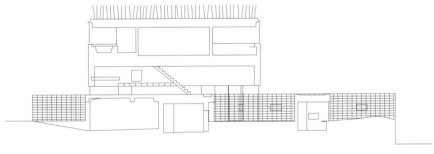

south–north

bathroom

bedroom

master bedroom · closet

elevator · bedroom

Japanese room

3F

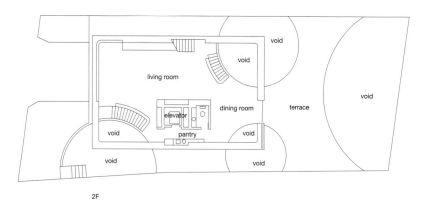

void

void

living room

void

void · elevator · dining room · terrace · void

pantry · void

void

void

2F

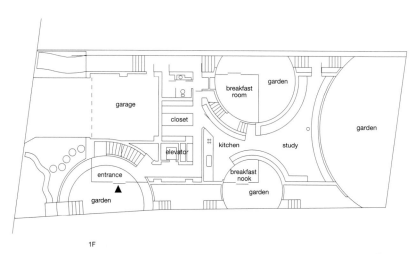

garage

breakfast room · garden

closet

elevator · kitchen · study · garden

entrance · breakfast nook

garden · garden

1F

Opposite top left: The breakfast room on the ground floor, with the dining room above it, occupies part of a circle that extends outside to enclose a small circular garden, another of the techniques employed for integrating the interior and exterior and visually expanding the space.

Opposite top right: A seemingly random pattern of lights and reflectors graces the ceiling. The large reflectors can be removed in order to access the ceiling for repairs or servicing without damaging the finishes. This is one of the several well thought out practical details seen throughout the house.

Opposite bottom left: Circular light holes have been located in a playful manner on the wall of the staircase leading from the living room to the third-floor bedroom area.

Opposite bottom right: The openings of a second set of light holes are visible on the outside wall leading to the roof terrace. Here, a sculpturesque steel staircase railing is a fitting finale to this unique house.

Left: The plans show the organization of spaces on the three levels. The garage, kitchen, breakfast room, study, and storage areas are located on the ground level. The next level contains the living, dining, and pantry areas. Three bedrooms, a *tatami* room, and a bathroom are located on the third floor.

Roundscape House

Architect Makoto Tanijiri, Suppose Design Office
Location Ohno Town, Hiroshima Prefecture
Floor Area 89.38 m² **Completion** 2004

Above: The façade of the Roundscape House faces the train tracks of Japan Railways and Setonaikai Bay in the distance. In contrast to the adjoining house lots where the sloping ground facing the tracks has been filled in, this house has been cantilevered over the slope. Exposed concrete was selected for the exterior in response to the harsh, salty air from the ocean.

Opposite: The outer shell of the southeast façade illustrates well the potential of concrete to be poured into any imaginable shape.

The owners of this house wanted a design that was minimalistic, but at the same time spiritually uplifting. In conjunction with the architect, they also decided that the various spaces of the house should not be separated from each other by hard walls, but instead be defined by the use of split floor levels, the size of the windows, and the height of the ceilings. The result is a delightful house that exudes a sense of harmoniously expansive space.

Located on a bluff above railroad tracks, the house overlooks a good view of Setonaikai Bay and Miyajima Island in the distance. Due to the harsh climatic conditions of the area, concrete was selected for the exterior of the house because of its corrosion-resistant qualities. Although widely used by architects since the middle of the last century, the artistic possibilities of concrete are seldom exploited for single-family homes. Here, however, the concrete has been poured into a sculpturesque shell that wraps around the various spaces of the house. Another innovation is the departure from the usual gray of the exposed concrete. This has been achieved by the application of a rust color stain to the concrete, making it far more inviting.

The various spaces in this house have been arranged in a sequence that starts from the relatively public spaces and leads to those that are more private. The entrance area, which comprises a piano studio and living room, is a light and active space. Walls set at different angles enhance the acoustical quality of the room. The level of privacy increases as one goes up half a level to the dining and kitchen area. A half flight of steps from here leads down to the master bedroom and the bathroom, while the other half flight of steps leads up to the second bedroom, the quietest part of the house.

The architect also believes in working with the natural environment of a site rather than protecting a house from it. His philosophy is exhibited here in the natural system of air circulation. Breezes coming in from the bay set up convection currents that flow through the whole house, escaping from the light and ventilation well in front of the second-floor bedroom, which also serves as a small terrace.

Opposite and above: The dining and kitchen areas (opposite) are accessed from the living room and piano studio (above) by a staircase with minimalistic treads, cantilevered out from the concrete slope that is part of the structural shell of the building. The staircase seen behind the dining table leads up to the second bedroom.

Left and below: The plans show the arrangement of the rooms on the lower level of the house and the second bedroom and adjoining terrace on the upper level.

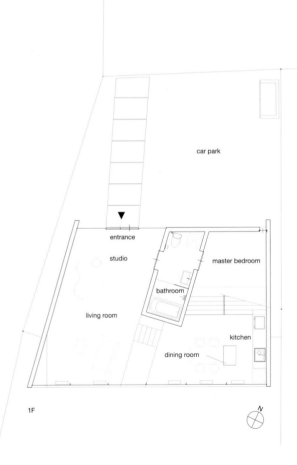

car park

entrance

studio

master bedroom

bathroom

living room

kitchen

dining room

1F

N

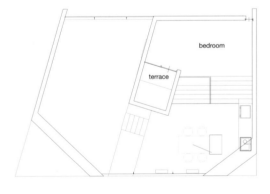

bedroom

terrace

2F

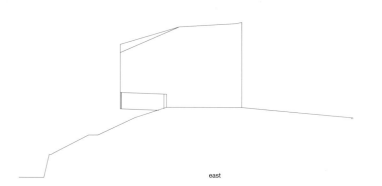

east

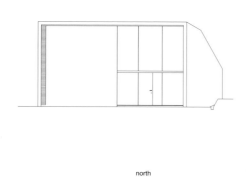

north

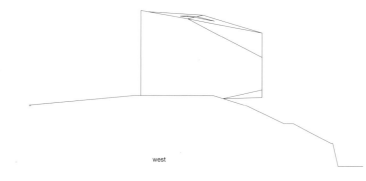

west

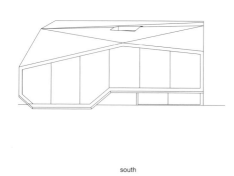

south

Opposite top left: The front entrance of the Roundscape House illustrates the contrast between the dark, rust-colored shell of the house, made of stained concrete, and the white walls and airy spaces within the house. The entrance path crosses a graveled area that also serves as a car park. Setonaikai Bay can be seen through the living room windows.

Opposite top right: Another minimalistic staircase leads from the dining area to the second bedroom on the upper level. The architect has consciously tried to replicate the spacious feeling of a traditional Japanese home by not partitioning the rooms in the house, including the bedrooms, with hard walls.

Right: The simplicity of the interior of the house is also carried through to the all-white bathroom.

Opposite bottom: The elevation drawings illustrate the way the house has been partially cantilevered above the slope of the site.

M House

Architect Katsufumi Kubota, Kubota Architecture Atelier
Location Iwakuni City, Yamaguchi Prefecture
Floor Area 138.17 m² **Completion** 2004

Above: The proportions of the house and its solidity lend it monumentality in spite of its small size. The few windows that punctuate the house, silhouetted here against the evening sky, have been kept small and glazed with frosted glass. Galvanized steel sheets have been used as siding material, adding to the monochromatic exterior.

Opposite: The specially constructed vaulted hallway on the ground floor leads up a wooden staircase to the second floor where the living and dining areas, and kitchen are located.

The owners of this house, in Yamaguchi Prefecture, wanted a place where they could always feel the presence of the river that flows nearby. The result is a remarkably peaceful home for the couple and their three children from which they can enjoy splendid views of the historical three-arched Kintai Bridge, the abundant greenery and cooling water, and also catch the fragrant breezes that flow over the site. In order to preserve the character of the area, recently enacted architectural laws require that all new buildings have a sloping roof with silver-black roofing material. This prompted the architect to use galvanized steel sheets for the siding of the house. The uninterrupted use of this monochromatic material on all façades gives the house a unique solemnity that is both monumental and somewhat reminiscent of old farmhouses in Japan. The windows that do not face the view have been kept small and are made of frosted glass.

A near perfect understanding between the architect and the owners on important issues relating to the site and the brief, enabled the design concept to be carried through with a minimum of change. The parties worked so well together that the architect found it hard to distinguish between their respective ideas on the completed design.

The rooms in the house have been organized on two levels. The main living and dining areas are located on the second floor to take advantage of the best possible views. These areas are reached from the entrance at the ground level through a straight, vaulted hallway that continues up a flight of wooden steps. The height of the vaulted ceiling meant that a special beam structure with joints had to be devised to avoid any interruption created by horizontal beams. Windows and openings are absent in this hallway, adding to its impact.

The monumentality of the house despite its small size is remarkable given that no special materials were used in its construction. This was in part achieved through the high-precision techniques that are conventional in wooden construction in Japan. All details were carefully worked out in advance and meticulously executed to avoid visual interruptions to the wall surfaces.

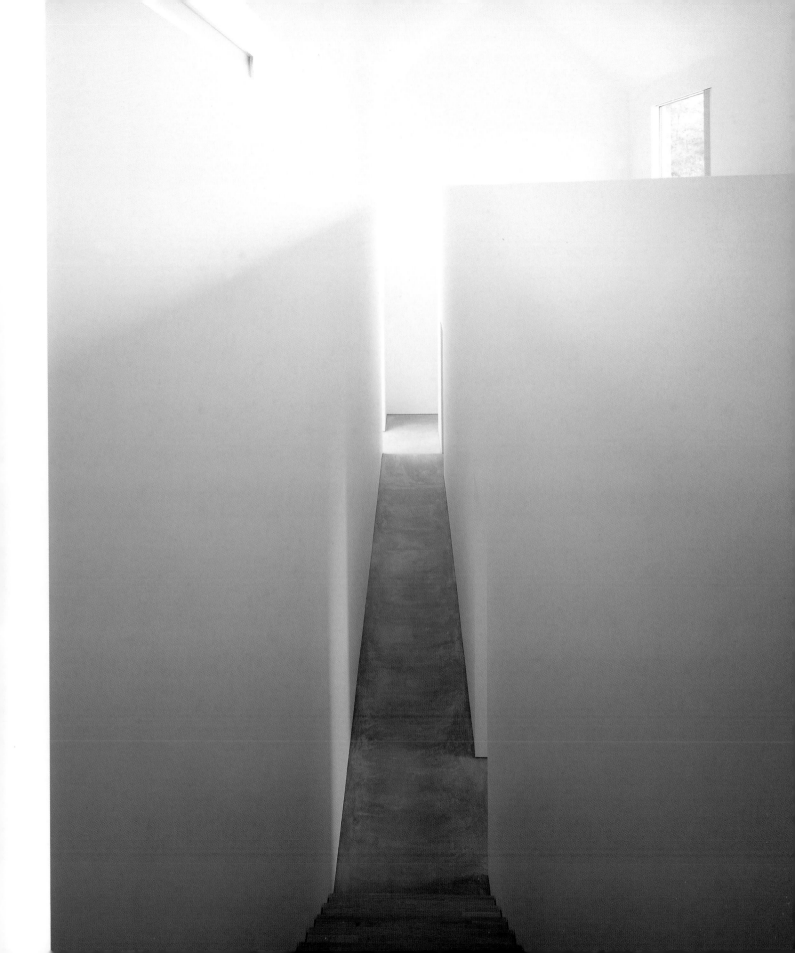

Left top: The living and dining areas, and kitchen are arranged within the farmhouse-like exterior. The form of the double-pitched roof makes a strong statement throughout the second floor, while the tall ceiling looming overhead and the walls, devoid of large windows, add to the solemnity of the lived-in spaces. Because of the height of the ceiling, a floor heating system has been installed for use in the winter months.

Left bottom: Light fixtures have been embedded on top of the staircase wall adjacent to the living areas. The staircase leads down to the bedrooms and Japanese room. The river and greenery are visible from the kitchen and dining area.

Above: The kitchen has a functional cooking island equipped with Gaggenau and AEG appliances.

Opposite bottom: The elevation drawings show the spaciousness of the building achieved by the restraint used in the location of door and window openings. The double-height entrance door adds to the monumentality of this small house.

Above: The chestnut wood flooring in the living room adds warmth to an otherwise minimalist interior. A large sliding glass door opens out to the terrace.

Above: The terrace in front of the living room, located above the bathroom wing, is covered with strips of water-resistant jarrah. A box-like structure on the terrace, part of the low wall that surrounds the terrace, houses a water faucet.

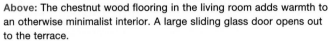

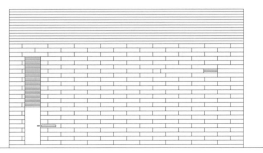

west

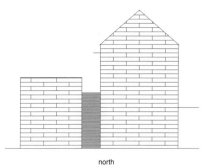

north

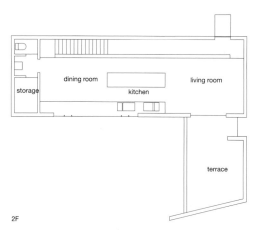

2F

Above: An all-white passage leads from the front entrance to the single-storied bathroom wing.

Right: The plans show the "flag-shaped lot" on which the various areas of the house have been arranged: the living and dining areas on the second floor of the main wing to catch the view of the nearby river, and the children's room, Japanese room, and master bedroom on the ground floor.

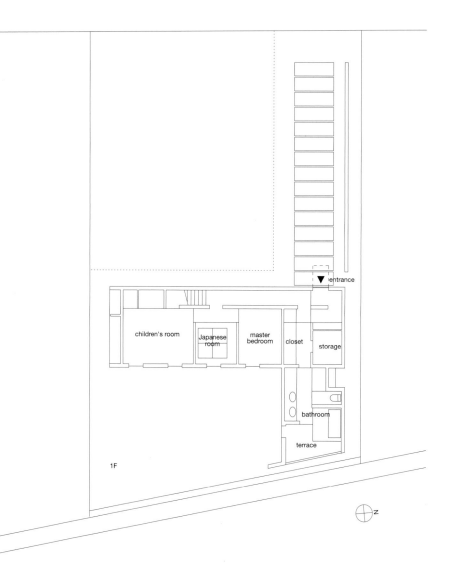

1F

Above: The glass and mosaic-tiled bathroom serves all the rooms on the ground floor. The washing area, used before entering the bathtub, is to the left of the tub.

Right: The Japanese room on the ground floor is covered with square Ryukyu *tatami* mats surrounded on all sides by a wooden board. These *tatami* mats, which lack the cloth borders of traditional mats, have become popular in recent years because of their simple design and sturdiness. Their origin can be traced back to the rush matting introduced from India to the Okinawa Islands a long time before *tatami* mats in their present form became ubiquitous in Japan. A modernized version of *Rikyu-mado*—a circular opening displaying the bamboo wattle of the traditional earthen walls in tea ceremony rooms—has been inserted in the lower part of the door leading to the garden.

Shima House

Architect Kazuhiko Oishi, Kazuhiko Oishi Architect Atelier
Location Itoshima District, Fukuoka Prefecture
Floor Area 179 m² **Completion** 2003

Is it possible to weave memories of good times and images from lifestyle magazines into your dream house? The answer, as seen in this house, is a resounding yes. At the beginning of the design process, the owners, a young professional couple in their thirties, passed the architect a CD titled "Shima Style" containing images scanned from magazines they had been collecting to show him the features they wanted incorporated into their new house. These included photographs of ocean views from wooden decks, barbeque parties with surfboards in the background, and outdoor showers with people washing off the sand after a day of surfing. The architect studied the CD carefully before coming up with a highly original design that accommodated the clients' lifestyle as well as captured the surrounding views.

The house, located on a hill in Shima in the northwestern part of Fukuoka Prefecture, has a seaside view of the Itoshima Peninsula on one side and mountains on the other. This picturesque location, which offers many opportunities for water sports, is not far from downtown Fukuoka City. For this reason, it is a popular residential area dotted with the homes of young professionals. The owners had been visiting this area every weekend to surf or party with resident surfers before finally deciding to relocate here from the city.

The visual organization of the house hinges on two bold L-shaped frames made of cedar wood using ordinary construction methods. Each frame comprises one long wall and a roof at a different height. The two opposing L shapes have been arranged in such a way that the vertical space between their rooflines has been left open to allow breezes and rain to come into the semi-enclosed areas of the house "without any architectural filters." One of the frames accommodates the living, dining, and kitchen wing, while the bedrooms are located in the other wing. Three open decks are included in the design for the enjoyment of the beautiful surroundings. The deck outside the living room looks out to the mountainside, while the one outside the audio room on the second floor has a view of the ocean. The third deck, located outside the bathroom, is fitted with showers for use after surfing.

Opposite: Japan is known for its simple but meticulous craftsmanship in wooden buildings. These traditions have been combined in the deck area between the living and bedroom wings with a modern and playful concept of space and contemporary materials such as steel posts. The space between the two overlapping roofs has been left open to the elements to heighten the sensation of living with nature.

Left: The audio room on the second floor is reached by a narrow staircase built into the side of the kitchen wall for stability. The staircase resembles the traditional Japanese *kaidan dansu* or staircase chest with storage built into it. The studio, defined by bold wooden beams and a glass railing, is a comfortable hideaway for the man of the house to enjoy his hobby: listening to ska and other music.

Below: The four elevations show the simple organization of the house. Its location on top of a slope allows for spectacular views, an asset which has been exploited in the open design of the house.

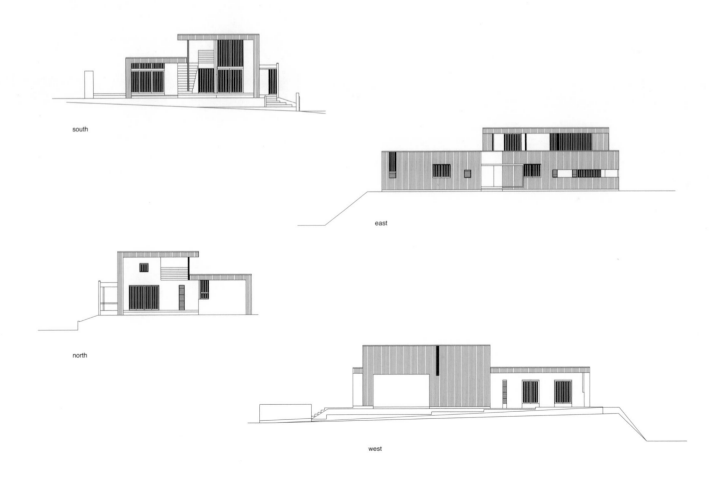

south

east

north

west

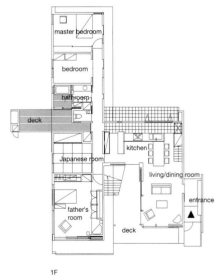

master bedroom

bedroom

bathroom

deck

Japanese room

kitchen

living/dining room

father's room

entrance

deck

1F

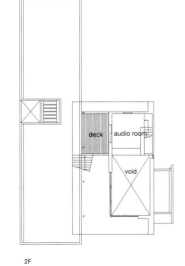

deck

audio room

void

2F

Opposite above left: The open-plan galley kitchen, designed for frequent entertaining, is well equipped with all the necessary appliances. The yard behind the kitchen opens out to the views and the breezes from the ocean. The bedroom wing is accessed via the deck glimpsed through the doorway.

Opposite below: The plans show the articulation of the house into two wings. The wing on the right accommodates the living, dining, kitchen, and audio rooms, while the one on the left has three bedrooms and a shared bathroom. The room for the father of the husband is at the front end of this wing, while the master bedroom is at the opposite end. A Japanese room has been included near the father's bedroom.

Opposite above right: The deck between the two wings and the staircase leading to the second floor are visible through the glass wall of the living room. Slender steel supports for the roof are playfully placed in the middle of the staircase treads.

Above: The clients' foremost requirement was that the house be designed for enjoyment of the beautiful natural environment surrounding the hilly lot. The architect thus created a house with as few barriers as possible to the ocean and mountain views: tall glass walls in the living and dining room, semi-open spaces under the overlapping roof, and three decks. Two bold, inverted L-shaped wooden frames, comprising the exterior walls and roof segments, define the house. Cedar wood has been used for the frame and deck flooring. Other than the warm hues of the wood, only black and white have been used in the interior.

Kunitachi House

Architect Chiharu Sugi & Manami Takahashi Plannetworks
Location Kunitachi City, Tokyo
Floor Area 203.73 m² **Completion** 2003

Above: The Kunitachi House is located on a long, narrow site in a high-density residential suburb of Tokyo.

Opposite: Different spaces in the house are defined by changes in level and by translucent acid-etched glass partitions. The three-dimensional printed design on the partitions creates dynamic patterns when juxtaposed with the light and shadows cast by the fiber-reinforced plastic (FRP) grating on the roof of the double-height dining room.

Located just a block away from the beautiful Kunitachi University Boulevard in a suburb of Tokyo, this house has been designed for a family of three. The architects were struck by the contrast between the lovely trees, the sidewalks, the bluebirds on the boulevard, and the visual clutter of the residential area, which has been steadily increasing in density due to the subdivision of lots. Mid-rise apartments are slowly replacing buildings along the boulevard, but individual houses behind them still carry some features of the original suburban development. The high floor area ratio allowed in the area means that views from a house usually consist of neighbors' fences and gates and, occasionally, a few trees. However, the height restriction away from the boulevard still assures penetration of plenty of sunshine.

The architects believe that a house should be connected to the outside even in a crowded neighborhood. With that in mind, they designed this house to softly filter and "edit" views from the house. Snippets of the sky or neighboring trees can be seen here and there as one moves inside the house. As far as possible, rooms for different uses have been separated from each other by a change of level, translucent partitions, and partially open walls.

The owners' requirements included a sunny child's room, a workroom that the whole family could use, an audio room, and a small *tatami*-matted room for *kitsuke*, the wearing of traditional kimonos. They also wanted a large room for displaying and storing their collections of Asian antiques and furniture. The interior spaces of the house have thus been kept simple in order to display and enjoy these collections. The interior finishes include exposed concrete walls, gray tiles, dark ironwood flooring, and light-colored wood.

Because of the small size of the lot, the house is staggered on several levels. The multilevel floors and walls with their large openings necessitated a reinforced concrete structural system. Plaster-coated external heat insulation has been applied on the concrete walls. Delicately textured double-glazing with a dot pattern has been used for added insulation. An underfloor heating system has been provided in most rooms.

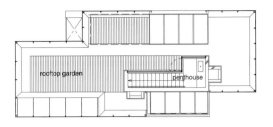

roof

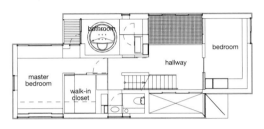

3F

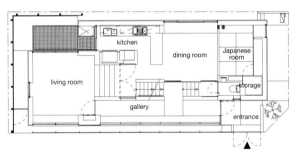

2F

B1F

Above and right: The kitchen, separated from the dining room by a counter, is equipped with specially imported appliances by Minotti of Milan. The counter top is made of 40-mm-thick Hokkaido stone, polished to a mirror finish. The edges of the counter have a rough hammered finish to contrast with the smooth top. Dark brown wood and frosted glass cabinet doors further complement the counter top and the ceramic tile flooring. A small outdoor area beyond the kitchen is enclosed with semi-opaque screens for privacy from neighboring houses.

Opposite left: The tiled main entrance, topped by a skylight, abuts the street and leads into the dining room, on a split level; this can be glimpsed through the window at the side of the steps. Such visual connections between different spaces, as well as glimpses of outside views, give the house a feeling of spaciousness. Acidetched double glass is used for the partitions throughout the lower level to provide privacy, while transparent glass on the upper levels allows views of the sky.

Opposite right: The plans show how the house is arranged along its narrow site. A basement contains the garage, storage, and a work studio for the whole family. The first floor has the living room and the open dining and kitchen areas as well as a Japanese-style room. The second floor contains the master bedroom suite and a smaller bedroom.

Above left: The bathroom of the master bedroom suite on the second floor is dominated by an extra large bathtub that can accommodate three people; it serves as the traditional Japanese *ofuro* in which families bathe together. Slate tiles cover the floor and glass walls enclose the shower area.

Above right: The large trees lining Kunitachi University Boulevard are visible from the penthouse, in a reference to "borrowed scenery," one of the main techniques employed in traditional Japanese garden design. A retractable skylight, which lets light and air into the dining room on the first floor through the FRP grating below, backs the penthouse. The decking outside the penthouse is made of ironwood.

Opposite: The staircase from the first floor to the second floor demonstrates how such diagonal lines, seen through glass and openings in the wall, add to the dynamic aesthetics of the house.

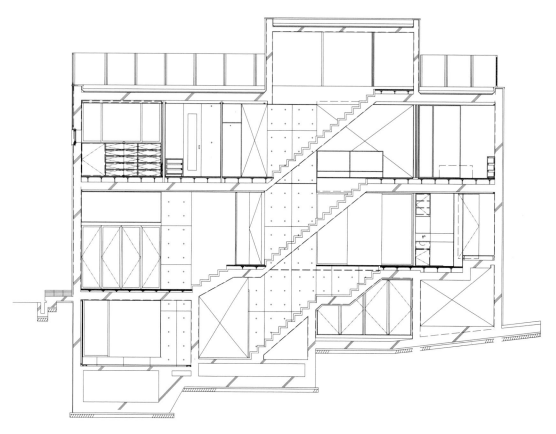

south–north

Above: The section drawings illustrate how a compact design can achieve a sense of openness with the use of partial or translucent walls and lines of sight across various levels.

Habikigaoka Residence

Architect Akira Sakamoto, Akira Sakamoto & Architects
Location Habikino City, Osaka Prefecture
Floor Area 208.72 m² **Completion** 2004

Hemmed in on three sides by other houses in a quiet but cluttered low-rise residential neighborhood, the Habikigaoka Residence exudes an aura of calm. The design of the 208-square-meter house, which is relatively spacious by Japanese standards, is not focused on getting maximum use out of its built-up area but rather on creating intimate spaces that induce a feeling of serenity. This is especially evident in the transitional spaces, such as the corridors and staircases. A good example is the main entrance to the house. While this space could have been designed as an entrance foyer leading directly into the living areas, the architect has, instead, placed a wall in the middle of this space, turning it into a softly lit double-turn corridor. From the main entrance one is led along the corridor to the focal point of the space: a small, square, low window through which one can see a Japanese-style garden just a few square meters in size. A partial view of a *mizu bachi* (water stone), moss, stones, and greenery is enough to be suggestive of a spacious tea garden. If this had been a full-length window, the boundary wall would have formed a large part of the view, and the small garden below would have lost its significance. After walking toward this window, one turns 180 degrees and is led toward another framed view, this time of the inner courtyard. The lack of ornamental distractions on the walls of the house, combined with the single-minded focus on the experience of walking through such spaces, is perhaps the most important and defining characteristic of the house.

In a manner reminiscent of traditional townhouses in Japan, the living spaces of the Habikigaoka Residence have been designed around an inner garden. The architect describes this as a "three-dimensional garden with a view of the sky." Besides the kitchen and living and dining rooms, a small *tatami* room has also been located on the ground floor at the request of the client. While this room is an obvious symbol of traditional influences, the whole house is, in fact, imbued with the traditional Japanese concept of space. The bedrooms are located on the second floor. The terraces on the second floor have also been designed as contemplative spaces, with parapet walls high enough to screen out the views and noise around them.

The exterior of the residence is composed of bold block-like volumes that articulate the spaces inside. In keeping with the owner's wishes, the exterior walls have been finished with white photo-catalyst paint. All technical fixtures have been built into the furniture, leaving the walls plain, further adding to the house's sense of calm.

Above and left:
The stark lines of the interior garden, shown in daylight (above) and at night (left), are softened by two trees. The decision to make the house face inward was based upon the lack of open space and pleasant scenery around the house. A sliding glass door in the living room provides access to the garden. The staircase leads up to the bedrooms on the second floor. The wooden deck at the right of the garden, enhanced at night with lighting, continues past the wall to serve as a utility space for the kitchen.

Above left: The small Japanese room on the ground floor is covered with Ryukyu *tatami* mats. The traditional full-height *oshire* cupboards meant for storing bedding in traditional *tatami* rooms have been reinterpreted here as a suspended closet with a frosted glass window below, matched by a larger frosted window to its right. An air conditioning unit and lighting fixtures have been built into the closet, contributing to the room's smooth, clean lines.

Above right: A narrow staircase leads up to the meditative terrace on top of the garage, surrounded by tall parapet walls, which offers a quiet retreat and a superb view of blue skies.

Right: The small, low window—the centerpiece of the entrance corridor— carefully frames a view of the garden outside, inviting the mind to imagine larger spaces. This window is reminiscent of the decorative alcove (*tokonoma*) found in traditional Japanese teahouses, which sets the mood for the room with a few symbolic flowers or a scroll painting.

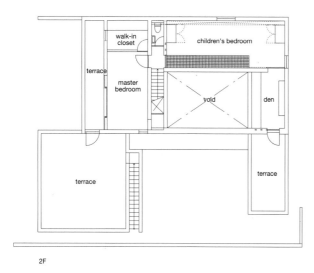

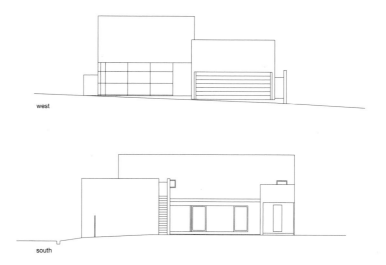

west

south

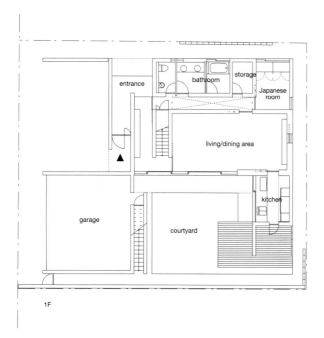

1F

N

Right and opposite: The den on the second floor looks out on to the upper part of the double-height living and dining areas below (opposite). At night, soft light from built-in lighting fixtures reflects on the white walls of the living/dining area, contributing to the feeling of spaciousness. The clean, block-like lines of the wood-burning fireplace echo the linear theme of the house. As far as possible, synthetic building materials have been avoided throughout. Components which come in direct contact with people, such as floors, doors, and railings, are all made of plain wood without the addition of chemicals.

Top and above: The plans and elevations show how the rooms of the house are arranged around the interior garden.

I House

Architect Katsufumi Kubota, Kubota Architecture Atelier
Location Hatsukaichi City, Hiroshima Prefecture
Floor Area 154.23 m² **Completion** 2004

Situated on a cliff across from the famous Itsukushima Shrine in the western part of Hiroshima Prefecture, I House symbolizes the owners' deep love of the ocean. The couple, who are avid scuba divers, had searched for a long time before they finally found this piece of land on the bend of a road that allows them spectacular sea views in three directions. The architect took this passion of his clients as the starting point of the design, and

combined it with what he calls the "inherent intent" of the sea cliff site.

The bold structure was conceived as a composition of concrete slabs, neatly folded like white sheets of *origami* paper that look as if they could float out to sea. The solid forms cradle simple minimalist spaces that open out on the seaward side. Exposed concrete, white painted metal, and glass form the interior finishes. Large glass walls on the seaward side have been kept clear of mullions, heavy columns, or messy details. Twice a day, when the tide is high, the house sits a bare four meters above sea level, giving it a magical feeling of being afloat on the ocean. At low tide, when the water drops another two meters, the scene becomes quite different. This extraordinary house is a nurturing anchor for the soul at all times and in all seasons.

Above: Although the front of the house is oriented toward the sea, its back (previous pages), facing the street, presents a composition of solid concrete forms.

Left top: The pool was designed to serve a dual purpose. The owners use it to rinse off seawater and sand when they return from their scuba diving trips. When not being used for this purpose, it serves as a *mizu niwa* (water garden), a small but important echo of the vast sea beyond.

Left bottom: The main entrance on the southwest side is set amid dynamically balanced planes of concrete and glass. The view from the terrace toward the living room underscores the simplicity of the design of the house. Circular structural posts of steel, painted white, have been set away from the glass surfaces so as not to impede the magnificent views. The living room is surrounded on two sides by large, single pieces of glass. The only solid wall in this room, made of exposed concrete, also stops short of the ceiling to allow the glass to wrap around its top. The wooden flooring of the living room is surrounded by the white finish of the terrace outside as well as the staircase landing.

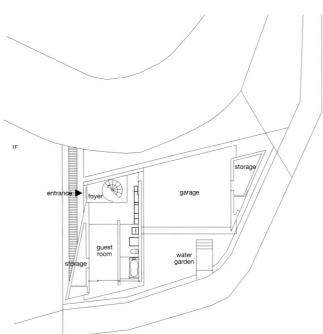

1F

entrance ▶ foyer

storage

garage

storage

guest room

water garden

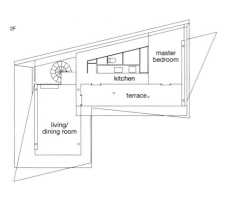

2F

master bedroom

kitchen

terrace

living/ dining room

Opposite left: An elegant spiral staircase leads from the main entrance to the second floor where the living and dining rooms, kitchen, and master bedroom are located. The white circular post supporting the staircase repeats the motif of the structural posts on the seaward side of the house. In addition to this entrance, an independent guest suite and the garage are located on the ground floor.

Opposite bottom and below: The plans and the elevation illustrate the geometry of the house as a response to the topography of the shoreline on one side and the street on the other.

Opposite right: The guest bathroom, with its exposed concrete walls and ceiling, looks out toward the sea and the oyster farms that are typical of the shoreline in this part of Hiroshima.

Right: Sunsets can be viewed through the glass walls of the living room, the razor sharp edges of the roof overhang and terrace floor adding dramatic effect to the scene. The kitchen and bedroom wing are visible on the left. Mullions for the glass walls have been concealed in the ceiling above and the floor below to enhance the feeling of oneness with nature.

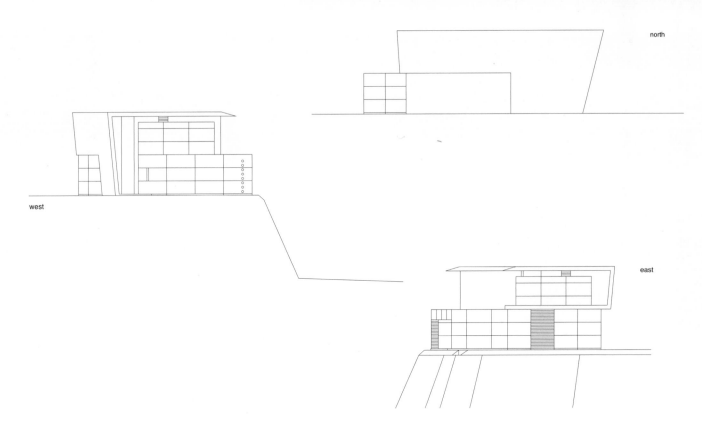

north

west

east

Karuizawa Gallery Villa

Architect Makoto Yamaguchi, Office of Makoto Yamaguchi
Location South Karuizawa, Gunma Prefecture
Floor Area 68.6 m² **Completion** 2003

Karuizawa is a premier vacation resort a mere hour away from Tokyo. It is popular with a mix of people: the young and the old, the wealthy and the poor, avant-garde artists as well as the literati. Even though new directions in art are constantly being tested here, this gallery villa stands out as truly being "out of the box," even by Karuizawa standards.

The clients did not adhere to the age-old philosophy of having a vacation home made of natural materials which would blend in with the wooded mountain surroundings. Instead, they wanted their villa to be made completely of hard, reflective, and inorganic building materials, and in particular specified that no wood be used for the finishes. The clients, both musicians, were looking for something exciting and timeless, rather than simply a practical and comfortable vacation house. Their main requirement was a flexible space that could work as a villa, a gallery for contemporary art (mainly sculptures), a salon for music concerts, and an amusing place to entertain friends.

The architect has translated the clients' requests into a simple hexahedron form made of reinforced concrete (RC) on wood, finished with white-painted fiber-reinforced plastic (FRP). The white paint finish on the interior walls has been complemented with other reflective materials, such as glass, mirror, and polished stainless steel. These materials work well together to create a flowing ambiguous, multiuse "white space" that is not meant for any preconceived purpose. This central space has been planned in a simple Y shape, that symbolically refers to the confluence of three lines used in "cross bearing," a method used for determining one's position in mountaineering or sailing.

The three arms of the Y shape extend out to glass walls that allow the flow of space from inside and out. The six points of the hexahedron thus formed connect at the triangular apex that shapes the ceiling and roof. The lower part of the hexahedron forms the base on which the gallery villa is lifted off the forest floor. All references to scale, on the inside or the outside of the house, have been avoided as far as possible, with the intention of making the structure appear like a scaleless "point" in the forest.

Above: Karuizawa Gallery Villa is situated on a steep mountain slope, with a southern aspect and good views of the forest. All the functions of the gallery villa have been neatly packed into a dramatic white hexahedron. Any references to scale, including in the landscaping, have been intentionally avoided.

Opposite: In the magical twilight of Karuizawa, the gallery villa softly glows through its various glass walls. The materials used on all parts of the hexahedron, including its walls, roof, and concrete base, combine to create a seamless form that appears to have floated down on to the site. The quality of stillness and minimalism achieved in the structure is not far from that of Japan's traditional teahouses.

Right: The angular geometry of the interior defines the character of the central space. This "white space" is meant to be adapted to various uses, such as a living area, a gallery for contemporary sculptures, or as a performance space for the musician owners. The floor is finished with mortar. The triangular space on the left serves as the bedroom and a secondary gallery.

Left: The reflectivity of the glass walls and luminous white painted walls help in visually dematerializing the wall surfaces.

Below: In the Y-shaped central space, the frames of the glass wall and doors have been concealed in order to avoid interruptions to the flow of space between the inside and the natural environment outside.

Above and left: The uninterrupted flow of white spaces has been so zealously pursued that even the bathroom, bedroom, and kitchen, located at the intersections of the Y shape (see plan opposite) are not divided into walled-in, private spaces. The bathtub (above), finished with mortar, is sunk into the floor and is given some modicum of privacy by a section of wall adjoining the main gallery space. Since the presence of a counter would have interfered with the flow of space in the kitchen (left), the counter has been inset flush to the floor. The person using the kitchen has to go down a few steps into a sort of narrow trench in order to prepare food at the counter at floor level.

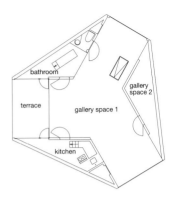

bathroom

terrace

gallery space 1

gallery space 2

kitchen

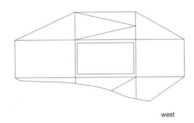

west

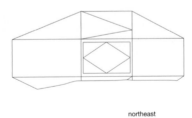

northwest

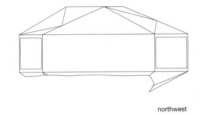

northeast

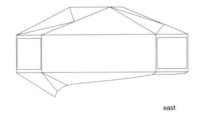

east

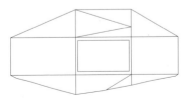

south

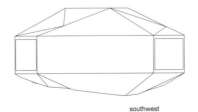

southwest

Karuizawa Gallery Villa was deliberately designed so that the usual elements of a house would be questioned and redefined. There is no formal front entrance, and the only way to enter the structure is through the kitchen or the bathroom. The usual separation of the areas of a house into private and public, or into those used during the day or at night, has been avoided. All areas, including the bathroom and the kitchen, are visually part of the multiuse "white space" at all times of the day and night.

TK House

Architect Makoto Shin Watanabe & Yoko Kinoshita, ADH Architects
Location Karuizawa Town, Nagano Prefecture
Floor Area 259.81 m² **Completion** 2003

Above: The southern face of the house in daylight. The placement of the house on the northern edge of the rectangular site, as well as the shape of the circular wooden terrace in front, which is made of *ipe*, a hardwood imported from Brazil, were driven by the desire to preserve as many of the existing trees as possible on the site.

Opposite: The living, dining, and kitchen areas are located within a semicircle, enclosed on the southern face by a straight window wall. The open kitchen is located to the left of the dining area. Access to the wooden terrace, with its attractive low railing, is through three sets of sliding glass doors. The white marble flooring complements the white walls and ceilings, enhancing the light and airy feeling. Designer furniture adds an elegant touch: the sofa set, named Veranda-3, and the coffee table, Sindbad, are from Cassina and were designed by Vico Magistretti; the dining table, named Athos, by Paolo Piva, and the Solo dining chairs, by Antonio Citterio, are from B&B Italia. The brass hood over the fireplace was salvaged from the couple's older house in Osaka when it was demolished.

Built as a retirement home for a couple in the resort town of Karuizawa, TK house has been shaped by three important factors: the environment, memories of the family's old home, and the experience of the owners while living overseas.

The beautiful natural surroundings in Karuizawa are hard for any sensitive architect or client to ignore. The owners had searched long and hard for an appropriate site before stumbling across this rectangular one, which has many mature trees and extends in a north–south direction. The house has been positioned on the northern edge of the site to enable the existing trees to be preserved and viewed from the south-facing glass wall of the central living spaces.

The second formative influence on the design of the house was the couple's admiration for the spacious homes they had seen in Europe and upstate New York during their long stay abroad. With these in mind, they requested the architects to create a double-height open-plan living/dining/kitchen area as the focus of their home. The outcome is an airy white living space with a window wall that brings the beauty of the woods into the interior.

Prized family possessions add a third flavor to the house. After the Kobe earthquake of 1994, the old family home (and birthplace) of the husband, which had been built in 1935 in Hamadera Park, Sakai City, Osaka, had to be demolished because of structural damage. However, several parts of the old house were saved and these were deftly incorporated by the architects into the new house. These salvaged elements include the doorknocker at the entrance, the wooden doors around the ground floor corridor, the Belgian stained-glass windows, and the brass fireplace hood in the living room.

Karuizawa's high summer humidity is an important design consideration. For this reason, a layer of charcoal has been installed under the floors, a remedy which has long been used in wooden temples in Japan to absorb moisture. For the cold winters, all areas except the guest bedroom are equipped with underfloor heating. This heating is supplemented with panel heaters concealed at the base of the tall living room windows and ceiling air circulators to circulate the warm air that rises in the double-height space.

Right: The living, dining, and kitchen areas are located within a semicircle, enclosed on the southern face by a straight window wall (page 155) and on the northern face by a solid arc-shaped wall lined with acoustical board to counter the reflective qualities of the large glass wall and marble floor.

Opposite: The kitchen area is tucked under the guest room, reached by a staircase curved to follow the shape of the wall.

Below: The plans show the geometric articulation of the semicircular living room in the overall trapezoidal form of the house. The arc of the living room wall has been extended outside the house to form the terrace. The library, main bedroom, and guest room are located around the double-height living core. Utility spaces are located on the north to protect the house from cold northern winds.

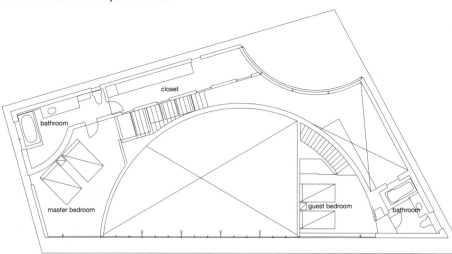

bathroom

closet

master bedroom

guest bedroom

bathroom

2F

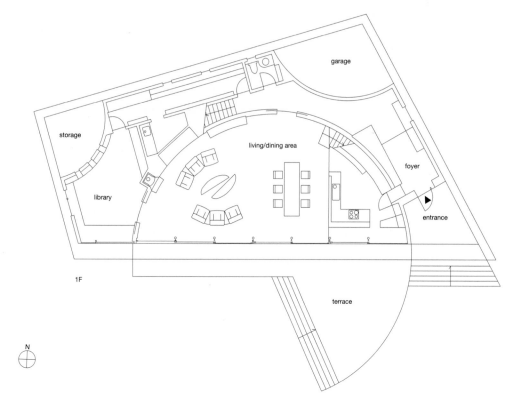

storage

garage

library

living/dining area

foyer

entrance

terrace

1F

N

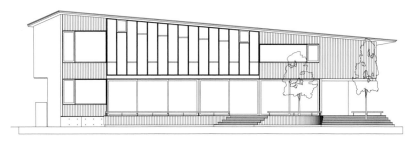

south

east

Opposite: The southern face of the house at dusk.

Above left: The master bedroom overlooks the wooded site beyond. The small table and chairs in front of the window were used by the owner in his childhood.

Above right: A view from the entrance foyer shows the inner corridor located between the main living core and the garage, library, and storage areas. The dark, oil-based stain on the plywood veneer in the corridor was specially selected to complement the Belgium stained-glass windows and the wooden doors retrieved from the family's old home in Osaka. The nostalgic ambience here contrasts with the white and airy living area.

Left: The drawings show the front and side elevations of the house.

Zaimokuza House

Architect Taketo Shimohigoshi
Location Kamakura City, Kanagawa Prefecture
Floor Area 82.78 m² **Completion** 2003

This house is located near the Zaimokuza coast in Kanagawa Prefecture. The coast and nearby town were given the name Zaimokuza ("timber place") when the area became a prosperous center of the wood trade during the Kamakura Period (1192–1333). Shipping and timber for house construction continued to be the mainstay of the economy in the area until the end of the Muromachi Period in 1573. The couple who own the house both work in the design industry, and they selected a corner lot at a time when the land around the house was still vacant. Since they guessed that the neighboring houses would most likely mimic an assortment of Western-style suburban homes, they opted instead for a strong contemporary design for their own place.

The house is a study in making small areas appear spacious through the use of glass walls, a complex inter-relation of multi-level spaces, and a restrained palette. Various activity areas have been organized on split levels along a spiral that wraps around an open core. These devices blur the separation of the two floors and create playful ambiguity and some measure of privacy for different functions of the house. Although the only view of the ocean is from the library window, the entire house is imbued with a sense of the ocean by the use of translucent gray-green interior glass walls and their reflection. The perception of space changes as the sun moves along the horizon, and electric lights are turned on. The color of the glass was of great importance to the design of the house, so its selection was put off until the very end while many different colors were tested. The spatial feeling of the house would indeed have been different if clear glass had been used.

Like many design professionals in Japan, the architect and the owners are great admirers of the work of the famous French architect Le Corbusier. The couple already owned the classic modern LC 2 leather and steel sofas that he had designed, and wanted to make sure these would fit in the new house. The architect has also fashioned the circulation pattern of this house in a counterclockwise direction, as was the case in the early houses designed by Le Corbusier.

Above: Decorative details and projections have been carefully avoided on the simple exterior of the house, in contrast to its more ostentatious neighbors, and the placement of windows gives no hint of the complexity of the spatial interior arrangements condensed into the neat cubic form.

Opposite: The kitchen is visible through the glass wall of the living room. The lighting fixture on the left, called Lucellino, was designed by Ingo Maurer in 1992, and is handcrafted from goose feathers. The INCISA chair by De Padova in the elevated library on the right, is another modern classic, and was designed by Vico Magistretti.

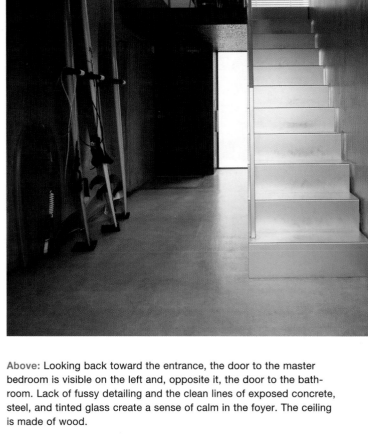

Above: The foyer has been designed like a *doma*, the informal space in a traditional Japanese farmhouse which usually had a packed earthen floor and was used by people to leave their shoes and heavy farm tools before entering the more formal parts of the house. In keeping with modern times, this space is used here for storing the owners' surfboards. The doors to the master bedroom and the bathroom are located past the foyer. The staircase, made of folded steel plates resembling crisp folded paper, is supported on a single exposed stringer beam.

Above: Looking back toward the entrance, the door to the master bedroom is visible on the left and, opposite it, the door to the bathroom. Lack of fussy detailing and the clean lines of exposed concrete, steel, and tinted glass create a sense of calm in the foyer. The ceiling is made of wood.

Right: The spiral spatial arrangement around the house's open core is defined by turns in the staircase leading to the upper floor. The living room and library are delineated by gray-green translucent glass walls that reflect each other. The sofa in the living room was designed by Le Corbusier in 1929, and was at that time called "the most famous chair of the century."

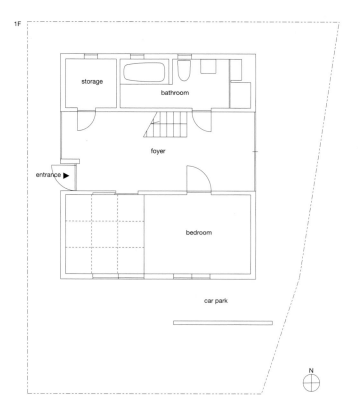

1F

storage

bathroom

foyer

entrance ▶

bedroom

car park

N

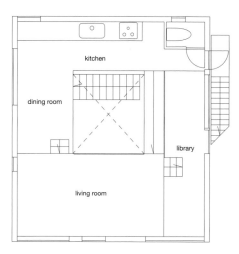

2F

kitchen

dining room

library

living room

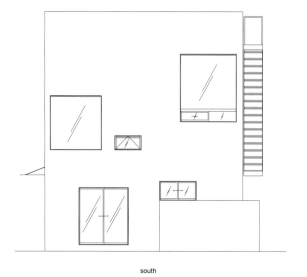

south

The plans of the house show how each space is located at a different level in a counterclockwise direction. Skillful design makes the total floor area of 82.78 square meters appear a lot more spacious than it actually is.

Right: The photograph here reveals how the various spaces, separated from each other simply by large sheets of gray-green glass, produce a kaleidoscope of reflections and views.

Kiyosato Gallery

Architect Satoshi Okada, Satoshi Okada Architects
Structural Designer Hirokazu Toki
Location Takane Town, Yamanashi Prefecture
Floor Area 207.10 m² **Completion** 2005

This house was designed as a vacation home for a couple with an extensive art collection. The architect commissioned believes that the design of any building is a synthesis of several factors. Of these, the first, spontaneous impression of the site is particularly important, even though one's initial response may be modified by subsequent thinking and reasoning. In this instance, the form of the Kiyosato Gallery was inspired by the impression of verticality of the larch trees and the oblong shape of the plot that the architect observed on his first visit to the site. The resulting tall, narrow structure, which faces the road, blends in with the trees around the site. In addition, the charcoal gray selected for the exterior makes the building almost invisible in summer among the dark shadows below the trees.

As one of his main design elements, the architect has used the concept of natural light entering a dim space. He maintains that although it is quite easy to fill a room with light, it is much harder to create dimness. He starts, therefore, by creating dimness. The next priority in his design process is to create fluidity of spaces. Rigid divisions between rooms are avoided so that the various spaces flow into each other. His awareness of the narrow site is revealed in his design of the interior where users are made to walk from one space to another via additional turns in the circulation system. Each turn along this path frames a different view of the outside or inside of the house, much like the principle behind traditional stroll gardens in Japan.

In response to the owners' limited budget, the house was built of wood, even though it was not easy to construct a house of this complexity using traditional building methods. The architect and engineer overcame the problem by developing an innovative system they refer to as the "Container Structure System (CSS)." This consists of putting specific functions of a house into boat-shaped container-like forms, which in turn act as structural supports. These elements include the stairs, storage, toilets, and kitchen. The spaces that remained in between these specific elements were considered fluid spaces, and it is these which accommodate all other functions of daily life.

Above and opposite: The slender shape and charcoal gray palette of the gallery, which faces the road, were chosen in deference to the stunningly tall and beautiful larch trees that populate the site. The rest of the house stretches beyond the gallery along the length of the narrow, sloping lot. Service areas have been designed in boat-shaped "containers" placed along the periphery of the house, with the living areas flowing in between. These service containers also serve as structural supports for the house.

Left: From the dining room a sloped passage on the left leads to the living room.

Below: An axonometric view of the house shows the wooden structural system with the "containers" acting as supports, an innovative solution to the problem of building such a complex structure from wood.

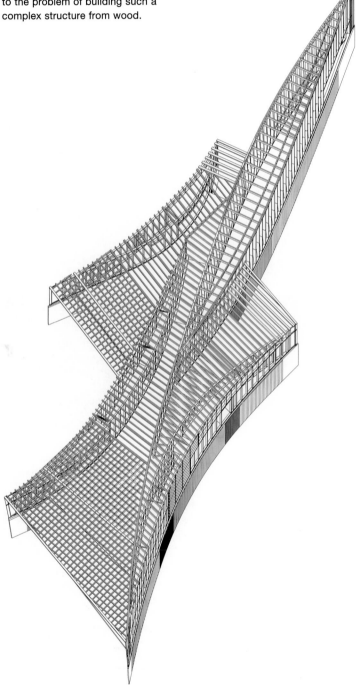

Above: A fireplace is set in the wall of the living room. Shadows cast by the trees through the glass doors add interest to the white walls and dark marble flooring.

Below: One end of the living room looks towards the narrow gallery wedged in the central boat-shaped "container," while the other end (not shown) faces a broad deck at the back of the house. The kitchen and dining room are on the right of the gallery while the passageway leading to the master bedroom is on the left. One of the two lofts in the house, where the couple's visiting children or other guests sleep on *futons*, is located above the dining room.

Above: The far end of the living room, the loft above it, looks out to a wooden deck. The gently undulating forms and the simplicity of the room's interior surfaces help to frame the beautiful surroundings of the house through the large double-glazed windows. A narrow, recessed window on the right provides a contrasting, cropped view of the landscape. The cowhide armchair and sofas in the living room are classics designed by the renowned architect Le Corbusier.

Right: A minimalist staircase in the gallery leads to the second loft. The drama of the natural light as it enters a dimly lit space is heightened by the curved walls of the narrow room.

Left: The deck outside the bathroom, at basement level, is visible through the full-length window.

Below: Visible from the rear of the house are the living room on the second floor and the bathroom suite below it. The slope of the site allowed the basement to be level with the ground, so that the bathroom can also open to a deck. Set further back on the left is the master bedroom and the stairs leading to its deck. The whole house is open to beautiful and inspiring views. The palette used on both interior and exterior surfaces—white, black, and charcoal gray—harmonizes visually with the deep shadows cast by the larch trees on clear days, while the juxtaposition of contrasting shapes and volumes—convex and concave, shallow and tall, long and compressed—heightens the awareness of the qualitative aspects of individual spaces.

The floor plans of the basement, second floor, and third floor reveal only too clearly how the architect has completely revolutionized the usual shapes of rooms. Stretched out along the narrow site, the rooms are connected to each other via the most picturesque route rather than the shortest path.

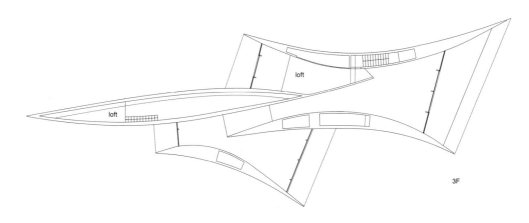

3F

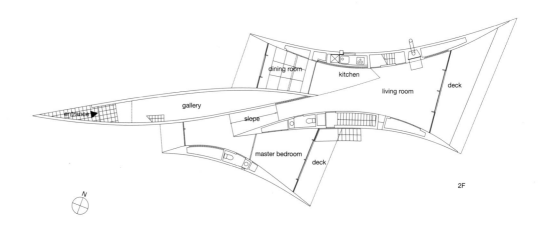

2F

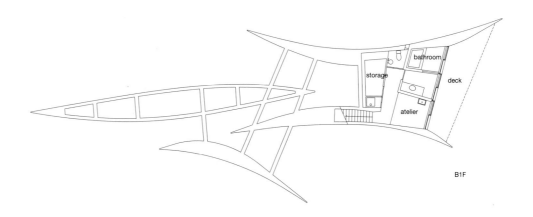

B1F

The Architects

Jun Aoki

Office Jun Aoki & Associates, #701, 3-38-11 Jingumae, Shibuya-ku, Tokyo 150-0001
Fax +81 3 3478 0508
E-mail info@aokijun.com
Url www.aokijun.com

Selected projects

1994 H (Katsuura, Chiba Prefecture)
1995 Mamihara Bridge (Soyo, Kumamoto Prefecture)
1996 S (Odawara, Kanagawa Prefecture)
1997 Yusuikan (Toyosaki, Niigata Prefecture), Fukushima Lagoon Museum (Toyosaki, Niigata Prefecture)
1998 Mitsue Primary School (Mitsue, Nara Prefecture)
1999 Snow Foundation (Yasuzuka, Niigata Prefecture), Louis Vuitton Nagoya (Nagoya, Aichi Prefecture), L (Tsujido, Chiba Prefecture)
2001 K (K City, Japan)
2002 Louis Vuitton Omotesando (Shibuya-ku, Tokyo), U bis, National Museum of Modern Art (Chiyoda-ku, Tokyo)
2003 Louis Vuitton Roppongi Hills (Minato-ku, Tokyo)
2004 Louis Vuitton New York (New York City), G (Meguro-ku, Tokyo)

Jun Aoki was born in Yokohama City in 1956 and received his MA from the University of Tokyo in 1982. He worked for Arata Isozaki & Associates from 1983 to 1990 before establishing Jun Aoki & Associates in 1991. His design for the Louis Vuitton flagship boutiques has earned him international acclaim. For each house Aoki designs, he randomly assigns a letter of the alphabet as its name. He is hoping to eventually design 26 houses, to cover the complete alphabet. His current projects include the Aomori Museum of Fine Arts, opened in 2006. The entire structure of the museum is placed in a large trench reminiscent of an excavation site. The museum's pre-requisite was the selective flow of traffic starting from the central exhibition hall, a brief that has clearly been accomplished. Over-hanging volumes are placed above the trench in a checkerboard pattern, creating alternating exhibition rooms and small spaces that provide visitors a choice of paths as they weave their way through the museum. Aoki has received numerous awards for his designs, including the Tokyo House Prize for "H" in 1994; the Kumamoto Landscape Award for Mamihara Bridge in 1996; the Yoshioka Award for "S" in 1997; and the AIJ (Architectural Institute of Japan) Annual Award for Fukushima Lagoon Museum in 1999. He has lectured at a number of universities, including the Japan Women's University and the Tokyo National University of Fine Arts and Music. The first compilation of his works, *Jun Aoki Complete Works [1] 1991–2004*, was published by Inax Publishing in October 2004.

Manabu Chiba

Office Chiba Manabu Architects, 3-54-4 Sendagaya, Shibuya-ku, Tokyo 151-0051
Phone/fax +81 3 3796 0777/ +81 3 3796 0788
E-mail www.chibamanabu.jp
Url www.chibamanabu.com

Selected projects

1994 Yoga House (Setagaya-ku, Tokyo)
1997 Wayo Seminar House (Sakura, Chiba Prefecture), Koto House (Koto-ku, Tokyo)
1999 Setagaya House (Setagaya-ku, Tokyo)
2000 Daizawa House (Koto-ku, Tokyo)
2001 House in Black (Ohta-ku, Tokyo), White Cube (Meguro-ku, Tokyo)
2002 split (Setagaya-ku, Tokyo), T-set (Setagaya-ku, Tokyo)
2003 S-House (Setagaya-ku, Tokyo), Kawada-cho Comfo-Garden (Shinjuku-ku, Tokyo), Trio (Setagaya-ku, Tokyo)
2004 DICE (Tanabe, Wakayama Prefecture), MESH (Setagaya-ku, Tokyo)

Manabu Chiba was born in Tokyo in 1960 and received his MA from the University of Tokyo in 1987. He worked at Nihon Sekkei Inc. until 1993 when he became a principal partner of Factor N Associates. He was appointed principal architect for the University of Tokyo Campus Planning Office where he served as a teaching associate for Tadao Ando. Chiba's philosophy of "exploring every possibility" is illustrated in his innovative treatment of materials and structural methods. The architect is not only well respected for his single-family home designs but also acknowledged for the recent success of his "high-design" rental apartments and cooperative housing. Currently an associate professor at the University of Tokyo, his work and essays have been featured in the TOTO publications entitled *Architecture of Tomorrow*, *Transferring of the Space*, and *10 City Profiles from 10 Young Architects*. As a faculty member of the University of Tokyo, he has also been involved in writing and editing *Le Corbusier Houses* and *World Architects in Their Twenties*. Chiba has received numerous awards, including Honorable Mention for the Japanese Cultural Center in Paris in 1990; the JIA (Japan Institute of Architects) Best Young Architect Award; the BCS (Building Contractors Society) Award and the Architectural Culture Award of Chiba Prefecture in 1998; the AIJ (Architectural Institute of Japan) Award in 1999; the Tokyo Residence Award in 2002; the Design Vanguard 2004; and the 21st Yoshioka Award.

Akihito Fumita

Office Fumita Design Office, Masa House 3F, 11-21 Sarugaku-cho, Shibuya-ku, Tokyo 150-0033
Phone/fax +81 3 5414-2880/ +81 3 5414 2881
E-mail info@fumitadesign.com
Url www.fumitadesign.com

Selected projects

1996 K-Two (Shisaibashi, Osaka)
1997 Free's Shop (Namba, Osaka)
1998 Inhale+Exhale (Kitano, Kobe)
1999 Natural Body (Namba, Osaka), Kikuchi Takeo Sculpture (Shibuya, Tokyo)
2000 Ete (Minami Aoyama, Tokyo)
2001 Nissan Gallery Ginza (Ginza, Tokyo), Nissan Gallery Headquarters (Ginza, Tokyo)
2002 Room in Bloom (Chuo-ku, Osaka), Star Garden (Shibuya, Tokyo)
2003 IXC. Collecta (Tamagawa, Tokyo), m,i,d,shop (Yurakucho, Tokyo)
2004 ANAYI (Shinjuku, Tokyo), Nissan Gallery (Sapporo, Hokkaido), M-premier BLACK (Nihonbashi, Tokyo)

Akihito Fumita was born in Osaka in 1962 and graduated from Osaka University of Arts in 1984. He worked for Ric Design until 1995, when he established his own studio in Osaka. He moved his studio to Tokyo in 1999. The house featured in this volume is Fumita's first residential project although he had already earned a reputation for excellence in retail design. He uses a "verbal filter" to transform his initial ideas into words, before expressing them as built form. The usual perceptions of elements such as walls and floors are then challenged and changed to arrive at a level of abstraction that invites personal interpretations from the viewers of his spaces. He discovers new applications for conventional materials that are contrary to their purpose, which is a distinct characteristic of his work. Fumita has received numerous awards, including the Grand Prix JCD (Japan Commercial Design) Award for Nissan Gallery Ginza in 2002; the Grand Prix Display Design Award and the Grand Prix Display Industry Award for Nissan Booth 35th Tokyo Motor Show in 2002; the Grand Prize Nashop Lighting Contest in 1997; and citations for the JCD Award in 1997, 1998, 1999, and 2002. His work has been featured widely in international publications, such as *eat.work. shop.:New Japanese Design*; *Design Japan: A New Vision of Contemporary Design Aesthetics*; *Space: Japanese Design Solutions for Compact Living*; and *Frame*. Prototype furniture and lighting fixtures designed by Fumita have been regularly exhibited at Tokyo Designer's Block since 2000.

Nobuaki Furuya

Office NASCA, Nihon Chusha Bldg. 4F, 3-15-1 Toyama, Shinjuku-ku, Tokyo 162-0052
Phone/fax +81 3 5272 4808/ +81 3 5272 4121
E-mail nasca@studio-nasca.com
Url www.studio-nasca.com

Selected projects

1990 Kogajo House (Kurose, Hiroshima Prefecture)
1994 Amakusa Visitor Center (Matsushima, Kumamoto Prefecture)
1995 Sendai Mediatheque Competition
1996 Yanase Takashi Museum (Kahoku, Kochi Prefecture)
1997 Waseda University High Tech Research Center (Shinjuku-ku, Tokyo)
1998 Waseda University Aizu Yaichi Museum (Shinjuku-ku, Tokyo), Baum Haus (Setagaya-ku, Tokyo), Poem and Marchen Gallery (Kahoku, Kochi Prefecture)
2002 Weekend House at Shui-Guan (Beijing, China), Il Cassetto (Fukuoka), Kondo Hospital, Hospice Tokushima (Nishi Shinhama-cho, Tokushima), Koenji-South Apartment (Suginami-ku, Tokyo)
2003 Kanna Nakasato Town Hall (Nakasato Kanna, Gunma Prefecture), Daita Apartment (Setagaya-ku, Tokyo)
2005 Chino Cultural Complex (Chino, Nagano Prefecture)

Nobuaki Furuya was born in Tokyo in 1955 and received his MA from Waseda University in 1980. He has been a professor at Waseda University since 1997. While a faculty member of Kinki University, he had the opportunity to travel to Switzerland as a fellow of the Agency for Cultural Affairs, where he worked for Mario Botta Architects from 1986 to 1987. Furuya established NASCA with Sachiko Yagi in 1994. Furuya believes in designing simple box-like spaces in which various rooms can be created simply by the addition of low partitions to suit the needs of the occupants. He sees flexibility as a necessary tool in enabling the occupants of a building to exercise their preferences. Furuya has received numerous awards, including the Yoshioka Award for Kogajo House in 1991 and the JIA (Japan Institute of Architects) Best Young Architect Award for Poem and Marchen Gallery in 1997. He has also received the AIJ (Architectural Institute of Japan) Award several times: for Yanase Takashi Museum in 2000; for Waseda University's Aizu Yaichi Museum in 2002; for Zig House/Zag House in 2003; and for Kondo Hospital in 2004. His work was exhibited at the GA Gallery in 1995, 1996, 1997, 1998, 2000, 2001, and 2003. A retrospective of his work, entitled "Shuffled," was displayed at Gallery MA in 2002, and another show, entitled "Eleven Agenda From Tokyo," was exhibited at the Japanese Bangkok Culture Center and at the National Museum Ulaanbaatar in 1995.

Shigemi Imoto

Office Imoto Architects, 7-4-1 Susakimachi, Hakata-ku, Fukuoka 812-0028, Fukuoka Prefecture
Phone/fax +81 92 273 1203/ +81 92 273 1236
E-mail imoto@alpha.ocn.ne.jp
Url www11.ocn.ne.jp/~imoto/

Selected projects

1993 Sun Terrace Imajuku (Nishi-ku, Fukuoka,), J House (Chuo-ku, Fukuoka)
1996 Gakuan (Chikushino, Fukuoka Prefecture)
1999 Shima Residence (Shima, Fukuoka Prefecture)
2001 Tani Villa (Chuo-ku, Fukuoka)
2004 U Residence (Nijo, Fukuoka Prefecture)
2005 K-House (Higashi-ku, Fukuoka)

Shigemi Imoto was born in Miyazaki Prefecture in 1953 and graduated from the Department of Environmental Design of Kyushu Institute of Design in 1979. Upon graduation, he participated in the Arcosanti Project, a non-profit educational project of the Cosanti Foundation founded by the Italian architect Paolo Soleri, located in the high desert of Arizona. In the late 1960s, Soleri had developed the concept of "arcology," a synthesis of architecture and environment, to explore alternatives in urban development in an age of environmental crisis. Greatly influenced by his experience in Arizona, Imoto's philosophy is to design "eco-human friendly" modern architecture using natural materials. After working for Noriyuki Miura Architectural Design Office for six years, he established his own practice, IMAI Associates, in 1985, renamed Imoto Architects in 1995. Imoto is the recipient of numerous awards, including the Fukuoka Prefecture Architecture and Housing Culture Award; the Fukuoka Prefecture Urbanscape Award; the 7th SD Review; and the Kumamoto Artpolis Prefectural Housing Competition. He was also selected for the 8th Nisshin Kogyo Competition. Imoto served as co-architect for the Dutch architect Rem Koolhaas and

American architect Steven Holl for Nexus, a large-scale urban development in Fukuoka City involving six international architects.

Katsufumi Kubota

Office Kubota Architect Atelier, 1-8-24 Imazu-cho, Iwakuni 740-0017, Yamaguchi Prefecture

Phone/fax +81 827 22 0092/+81 827 22 0079

E-mail webmaster@katsufumikubota.jp

Url www.katsufumikubota.jp

Selected projects

1993 Crystal Unit (Obatake, Yamaguchi Prefecture)

1996 Crystal Unit II (Iwakuni, Yamaguchi Prefecture)

1998 Crystal Unit III (Hiroshima, Hiroshima Prefecture)

1999 Y-House (Iwakuni, Yamaguchi Prefecture)

2000 N-House (Iwakuni, Yamaguchi Prefecture)

2001 Yamaguchi Prefecture Pavilion (Ajisu, Yamaguchi Prefecture)

2005 M-Clinic (Hiroshima, Hiroshima Prefecture)

Katsufumi Kubota was born in Yamaguchi Prefecture in 1957 and graduated from the Faculty of Architecture and Engineering at Nihon University in 1981. On graduation, he worked at K Constructural Institute until 1988 when he established Kubota Architect Atelier. He has also taught at Yamaguchi University since 2000. Kubota's architectural work focuses on creating abstract spaces which he refers to as "nothingness." He strives to carefully study and design the details of his buildings based upon the relationship between various construction materials. Environmental factors such as sunlight and the flow of air play a great role in his designs. Kubota's ultimate goal is to enhance the quality of daily life of his clients. He has received numerous awards, including the Grand-Prix Hiroshima Future Design in 1997; the United Nations Human Settlements Program (Habitat) Japanese Project Award in 1998; First Prize for the Yamaguchi Expo Kirara Pavilion Competition in 2001; Final Short-Listed Nominee for the World Architectural Awards in 2002; and Special Prize for the Dedalo Minosse International Prize in 2004. His works have been widely featured in international publications such as *Houses on the Edge*, *Minimalism*, *Minimalist Houses*, *Casabella*, *PreFab*, *GA Houses*, and *Architectural Digest*.

Shinichi Ogawa

Office Shinichi Ogawa & Associates, 5-33-18 Inokuchi, Nishi-ku, Hiroshima 733-0842, Hiroshima Prefecture

Phone/fax +81 82 278 7099/+81 82 278 7107

E-mail info@shinichiogawa.com

Url www.shinichiogawa.com

Selected projects

1989 Cubist House (Yamaguchi)

1991 Restore Station (Hiroshima Prefecture)

1995 Hatsuta Yamaguchi Corporation (Yamaguchi Prefecture)

1996 Isobe Studio & Residence (Yamaguchi), Kid Museum (Yamaguchi Prefecture), Glass House (Hiroshima)

1997 Nagaya Ladies Clinic (Yamaguchi)

1998 White Cube (Hiroshima)

1999 Cassina ixc. Hiroshima (Hiroshima)

2001 Tunnel House (Hiroshima)

2002 Barbas (Yamaguchi), 104X (Yamaguchi)

2003 K house (Tokyo)

2004 Court House (Saitama Prefecture), Loft House (Nagoya)

Shinichi Ogawa was born in Yamaguchi Prefecture in 1955. He received his BFA from Nihon University in 1978 after studying architecture at Washington State University on a scholarship. As a fellow of the Agency for Cultural Affairs run by the Japanese Government, he traveled to New York in 1984 where he worked with Paul Rudolph Architects and Arquitectonica. He established his own practice in 1986 after returning to Japan. He is currently a professor at Kinki University and a visiting professor at the Edinburgh College of Art. Simple shapes and "elimination of the inessential" define Ogawa's architectural work. His minimalist, box-like residences provide maximum flexibility to accommodate the diverse daily activities of the occupants. He is the recipient of numerous awards, including the SD Award in 1989, 1990, 1991, and 1992, and the Gold Prize for the CS Design Award. He received an honorary mention in the Yokohama International Port Terminal Competition in 1995, and the Scottish Architecture and Design Center Competition in 1996. His work has been exhibited on several occasions, including at the Milano Triennale Japanese Pavillion in 1996; the "Japan Year 2001 London 4x4x4 Japanese Avant-Garde"; and the Gwanju Biennale in 2002. A retrospective of his works was held at the Hiroshima City Museum of Modern Art in 2004. His work has also been published in *SD Special Feature: Shinichi Ogawa*, *Transbody*, *10x10*, *The House Book*, and *Modern House*.

Kazuhiko Oishi

Office Kazuhiko Oishi Architecture Atelier, 7-2-7 Nishijin, Sawara-ku, Fukuoka 814-0002, Fukuoka Prefecture

Phone/fax +81 92 823 0882/+81 92 823 0925

E-mail oishi.architect@jcom.home.ne.jp

Url www.members.jcom.home.ne.jp/oishi.architect/

Selected projects

1997 Clinic K (Kokura, Fukuoka Prefecture)

1998 F (Yahata, Fukuoka Prefecture), Hospital K (Kurume, Fukuoka Prefecture)

1999 Hojunkyo (Sawara-ku, Fukuoka)

2000 Seaside House (Itoshima, Fukuoka Prefecture)

2001 Clinic Y (Kokura, Fukuoka Prefecture), Naya (Dazai-fu, Fukuoka Prefecture)

2002 CITY CUBE (Sawara-ku Fukuoka, Fukuoka Prefecture)

2003 M Residence (Yahata, Fukuoka Prefecture), O Clinic (Chikugo, Fukuoka Prefecture)

2004 Fabric Wall Residence (Hakata-ku, Fukuoka), HOUSE N (Minami-ku, Fukuoka)

2005 White in Gray (Ogori, Fukuoka Prefecture), R (Sawara-ku Fukuoka)

Kazuhiko Oishi was born in Fukuoka Prefecture in 1956 and in 1978 graduated from the Department of Environmental Design of Kyushu Institute of Design. On graduation, he worked for Mamoru Yamada Architects from 1978 to 1994. In 1995, he established his own practice, Kazuhiko Oishi Architecture Atelier. Oishi seeks to create architecture that enhances the interaction between the occupants of a building and their surroundings through what he refers to as an "abstracted filter of nature."

He introduces natural phenomena such as rain, fog, sunsets, and ocean breezes into the interior of a building in order to create a special environmental experience. He is the recipient of the Fukuoka Prefecture Housing Culture Award in 2002, the year in which he also earned a Commendation in the Tokyo Gas Housing Competition Award for City Cube. Currently a lecturer at Kinki University and Kyushu Industrial University, Oishi's work has been featured in international publications such as *House Design* and *Pacific Houses*.

Satoshi Okada

Office Satoshi Okada Architects, 1-6-31-4F Higashi, Kunitachi, Tokyo 186-0002

Phone/fax +81 42 505 5065/+81 42 505 5066

E-mail mail@okada-archi.com

Url www.okada-archi.com

Selected projects

1991 Una Porta per Venizia, Venice Biennale

1992 Installation of "Time," Spiral Building (Aoyama, Tokyo), The Urban Ring, Yokohama Urban Design Competition

1995 House in Kami-Asao (Kawasaki, Kanagawa Prefecture)

1997 villa man-bow (Atami, Kanagawa Prefecture)

2000 House in Mt Fuji (Minami-tsuru, Yamanashi Prefecture), House in Matsubara (Matsubara, Osaka Prefecture)

2001 House in Hakone (Hakone, Kanagawa Prefecture)

2002 House in Togoshi (Shinagawa-ku, Tokyo)

2003 House in Takaban (Meguro-ku, Tokyo), House in Sakakida (Kita-ku, Kyoto), House in Takanawa (Minato-ku, Tokyo), House in Eda (Eda, Hiroshima Prefecture)

2004 House in Hanegi (Setagaya-ku, Tokyo), House in Todoroki (Setagaya-ku, Tokyo)

Satoshi Okada was born in Hyogo Prefecture in 1962 and graduated from the Graduate School of Architecture, Planning, and Preservation at Columbia University in 1989. As a fellow of the Japan Society for the Promotion of Science and the National Fellow of Artists, he did research work under Professor Kenneth Frampton at Columbia. After returning to Japan in 1995, he established his own practice. Okada's work garnered international acclaim with House in Mt Fuji, a black diagonal volume nestled in moss-covered terrain, which was figuratively labeled by the architect himself as "a shadow in the forest." Contrasts of light and shadow and of spatial dimensions are the central themes that epitomize his work. Entrance halls and stairs are often tall, narrow, and dark spaces accentuated by a single slit of light, that lead into expansive, light-filled spaces. Currently an associate professor of the School of Environmental Design at the University of Shiga Prefecture, he has been involved in organizing new academic programs. He has also established the DIEA (Design Institute for Environmental Architecture) for promoting design activities in natural environment and regional communities. He serves as a visiting lecturer at numerous international institutions, including La Basilica Palladiana in Vicenza, University of Vienna, ETH in Zurich, and Politecnico di Milano. His designs have been published widely in international publications, including *20 architetti per Venti Case*, *Minimalist Spaces*, *Houses on the Edge*, *Case di Vacanza*, *World Houses*, and *Architecture of the New Millennium*.

Akira Sakamoto

Office Akira Sakamoto Architect & Associates, 1-14-5 Minamihorie Nishi-ku, Osaka 550-0015

Phone/fax +81 6 6537 1145/+81 6 6537 1146

E-mail casa@akirasakamoto.com

Url www.akirasakamoto.com

Selected projects

1995 Creo Hall (Toyama, Toyama Prefecture)

1996 Hakuei Residence (Minoh, Osaka Prefecture), House in Tondabayashi (Tondabayashi, Osaka Prefecture), House in Kitakusu (Daito, Osaka Prefecture)

1998 Light Hall Echigo (Toyama, Toyama Prefecture), House in Sayama (Sayama, Osaka Prefecture)

1999 Hakuu-kan (Fujiidera, Osaka Prefecture)

2000 Atelier in White (Osaka), House in Aobaku (Yokohama)

2002 Hakusetsu Dental Clinic (Toyama, Toyama Prefecture)

2003 House in Kyoto (Kyoto), House in Umegaoka (Setagaya-ku, Tokyo), House in Fukazawa (Setagaya-ku, Tokyo)

2004 Sesami Restaurant (Osaka)

2005 House in Kashiba (Kashiba, Nara Prefecture)

Akira Sakamoto was born in Fukuoka Prefecture in 1951. He worked at Kinki Architecture and Structure Laboratory before establishing his own architectural practice in 1982. He currently lectures at Kinki University, Kansai University, Kyoto Prefectural University, and Osaka Institute of Technology. His block-like white volumes are a welcome presence in residential areas strewn with obtrusive houses. In response to unfavorable residential sites, Sakamoto designs living spaces around inner gardens to allow a view of the sky while protecting the privacy of the occupants from neighboring houses. His signature design features include skylights installed above hallways and stairs, and diminutive tea gardens wedged between small spaces. Sakamoto is the recipient of numerous awards, including the Grand Prize for the Nashop Lighting Contest in 1995 and 2004; the Grand Prize for the Takaoka City Urbanscape Award in 2003; the AIJ (Architectural Institute of Japan) Award in 2001 and 2003; the Grand Prize for the Japan Architects Confederation in 2001; the Osaka Governor Award, and the JIA (Architectural Institute of Japan) Best Young Architect Award in 1997. His works have also been featured in international publications: on the cover of *Minimalist Interiors*, and inside *Loutus*, *Award Winning Architecture*, *Single Family Homes*, *GA House 50*, and *GA Japan*. His designs were exhibited in "Japan Total Towards Totalscape" (Netherlands Architect Institute) in 2001, and in "Sensai–Japanese Architecture" (National Architecture Museum of Mexico) in 2004.

Taketo Shimohigoshi

Office A.A.E. (Associates of Architecture and Environment), 2-24-36-2F Nishi-azabu, Minato-ku, Tokyo 106-0031

Phone/fax +81 3 6805 1240/+81 3 6805 1241

E-mail studio@aae.jp

Url www.aae.jp

Selected projects

1998 Obuse House (Obuse, Nagano Prefecture), Kita-Aoyama Apartment Building (Minato-ku, Tokyo)

2001 Shiromeguri House (Kamakura, Kanagawa Prefecture), Inden-Ya Aoyama Shop (Minato-ku, Tokyo), Inden-Ya Shinsaibashi Shop (Shinsaibashi, Osaka)

2003 Wakanoura Art Cube (Wakanoura, Wakayama Prefecture)

2004 Inden-Ya Kofu Shop (Kofu, Yamanashi Prefecture)

2005 FLEG Daikanyama (Shibuya-ku, Tokyo)

Taketo Shimohigoshi was born in Hiroshima Prefecture in 1965 and received his MA from Yokohama National University in 1990. From 1990 until 1997 he worked for Atsushi Kitagawara Architects, before leaving to establish his own practice, A.A.E. He currently lectures at Hosei University and Waseda University. Shimohigoshi confesses that his designs are fueled by a simple desire to experience novel spaces. He thus attempts to approach each project with refreshing, new design ideas as breakthrough solutions to site conditions and client requirements. The gray-green tinted thermal glass and the meticulous detailing for its installation in the house featured in this volume are illustrations of such solutions. Shimohigoshi was commissioned to build an artist-in-residence studio based on his award-winning design in the Wakanoura Art Cube Design Competition, 2002. Other awards he has received include nomination for the 22nd Inax Design Competition for Obuse House in 1999; the Encouragement Award for the 49th Kanagawa Architectural Competition for Zaimokuza House in 2004; the Good Design Award for Wakanoura Art Cube in 2004; and the AIJ (Architectural Institute of Japan) Annual Architectural Design Commendation in 2005. His work has been featured in Japanese publications such as *Shinkenchiku*, *Kenchiku Chishiki*, *Pen*, and *GA Japan*.

Takao Shiotsuka

Office **Takao Shiotsuka Atelier, 301-4-1-24 Miyako-machi, Oita, Oita Prefecture 870-0034**

Phone/fax **+81 97 538 8828/+81 97 538 8829**

E-mail **shio-atl@shio-atl.com**

Url **www.shio-atl.com**

Selected projects

1997 Tsukumi House (Tsukumi, Oita Prefecture)

1999 Genkai Weekend House (Genkai, Fukuoka Prefecture), Kinda (Mie, Oita Prefecture), Kunimi Cultural Factory MINNANKAN (Kunimi, Oita Prefecture)

2001 hairdresser F (Beppu, Oita Prefecture)

2002 Kitsuki Residence (Kitsuki, Oita Prefecture), Ohno Bus Terminal (Ohno, Oita Prefecture), Private Gallery (Oita, Oita Prefecture), Shigemi House (Oita, Oita Prefecture)

2003 hair salon S (Oita, Oita Prefecture), furniture shop CICOU (Oita, Oita Prefecture)

2004 Shin Oita 2-Bldg. (Oita, Oita Prefecture), atu house (Onojo, Fukuoka Prefecture), Banquet Hall (Oita, Oita Prefecture), Blue House (Saiki, Oita Prefecture)

Takao Shiotsuka was born in Fukuoka Prefecture in 1965 and received his MA from Oita University in 1989. He worked for Archaic Architects from 1989 to 1993 before establishing his own practice in 1994 in Oita City. Shiotsuka has opted to stay and work in Oita because he prefers hands-on involvement in his projects. The diverse range of his projects includes parks, residences, a bus terminal, hair salons, commercial buildings, and community centers. All of these are located in Kyushu, mostly in Oita Prefecture. Sloping walls and roofs are signature design features of his work and resemble the mountainous landscape of Kyushu. Shiotsuka is especially interested in the connection between his architecture and its natural surroundings. Shiotsuka received the Good Design Award for Kunimi Cultural Factory MINNANKAN in 2001 and the Special Prize of the International Design Competition for Northern Style Housing Complex in Aomori in 2002. His work has been featured in international and local publications such as *New Kitchen Design*, *Wallpaper*, *Hauser*, *Architectural Record*, *Space*, and *Shinkenchiku*. His work was also exhibited in "New Architecture in Japan and Poland" at Manggha Japan Culture and Technology Center in Krakow, Poland, in 2004.

Chiharu Sugi & Manami Takahashi

Office **Plannet Works, Hillside Terrace A/3, 29-18 Sarugaku-cho, Shibuya-ku, Tokyo 150-0033**

Phone/fax **+81 3 5459 1360/+81 3 5459 1242**

E-mail **plannet@fd.catv.ne.jp**

Url **www.plannetworks.jp**

Selected projects

1997 Yamatocho House (Nakano-ku, Tokyo)

1998 Noa 1998 (Taito-ku, Tokyo)

1999 Sai Market (Itabashi-ku, Tokyo), Forest House (Kitakoma-gun, Yamanashi Prefecture)

2001 Air Alley (Machida-shi, Tokyo)

2002 Minami Aoyama Cooperative (Minato-ku, Tokyo), House in Saginomiya (Nakano-ku, Tokyo)

2003 House in Nanokahara (Zao, Miyagi Prefecture)

2004 Seta III Cooperative (Setagaya-ku, Tokyo), House in Oyamadai (Setagaya-ku, Tokyo)

2005 Jingumae Project (Shibuya-ku, Tokyo), Nampeidai A Project (Shibuya-ku, Tokyo), House in Kohoku (Tsuzuki-ku, Yokohama), Kotake Sai House (Itabashi-ku, Tokyo), Mable Apartment (Meguro-ku, Tokyo)

Chiharu Sugi was born in Akita Prefecture in 1958 and graduated from the College of Art at Nihon University in 1981. He worked at Kenchiku Design Studio from 1981 until 1996. He currently lectures at Nihon University, Kanto Gakuin University, and Tokyo Denki University. Manami Takahashi, born in Tokyo in 1959, graduated from the School of Architecture of Tokyo National University of Fine Arts and Music in 1984. She also worked at Kenchiku Design Studio, from 1984 until 1996, and lectures at Tokyo National University of Fine Arts and Music, School of Architecture and Tokyo Denki University. In 1996, Sugi and Takahashi established a joint practice under the name Plannet Works, specializing in residential design for single-family and cooperative housing. In their designs, they often make use of *shakkei* ("borrowed scenery"), a traditional technique employed in Japanese landscape design in which mountains and buildings that lie outside the garden are incorporated into the design of the garden. The two architects believe that architectural walls, whether constructed of heavy concrete or thin membranes, define one's consciousness of place and demarcate it from its surroundings. Plannet Works' designs aim to help people avoid a sense of alienation by making them feel connected to views of the surrounding environment and cityscape.

Makoto Tanijiri

Office **Suppose Design Office, 13-2 Kako-machi, Naka-ku, Hiroshima 730-0812**

Phone/fax **+81 82 247 1152/+81 82 247 1152**

E-mail/url **info@suppose.jp/www.suppose.jp**

Selected projects

2001 Koi House (Nishi-ku, Hiroshima)

2002 REGO Building (Naka-ku, Hiroshima)

2003 Bishamon House (Asaminami-ku, Hiroshima), Otoya (Miyoshi, Hiroshima Prefecture)

2004 Kuchita Building (Kita-ku, Hiroshima), Ujina House (Minami-ku, Hiroshima), Kurashiki Hamacho House (Kurashiki, Okayama Prefecture), Hijiyama House (Minami-ku, Hiroshima), Yakeyama House (Kure, Hiroshima Prefecture), Kameyama House (Asakita-ku, Hiroshima Prefecture), Ushitashinmachi House (Higashi-ku, Hiroshima), Ohno House (Ohno-cho, Hiroshima)

2005 Kurashikioki House (Kurashiki, Okayama Prefecture), House in Hiratsuka (Hiratsuka, Kanagawa Prefecture)

Makoto Tanijiri was born in Hiroshima Prefecture in 1974. He worked for Motokane Architect Office from 1994 to 1999 and HAL Architect Office from 1999 until 2000, when he established his own practice. The staff of Suppose Design Office, which includes four other young architects besides Tanijiri, are currently working on over twenty projects, mostly in Hiroshima Prefecture. These include single-family homes, restaurants, and commercial buildings. The company's architects bring new, creative, and experimental approaches to each of their projects, a good example of which is Tanijiri's award-winning Bishamon House. This house was designed as a large, bold, transparent box perched on a steel A-frame on top of a hill. The steel legs which support the box-shaped building are suggestive of a great mountaintop swing. The building's thin and free-floating slabs, glass walls, and minimalist railings all contribute to a feeling of excitement, while the solid forms of the exposed steel A-frame provide a sense of security. Tanijiri has received numerous awards, including the JCD (Japan Commercial Design) Award in 2002, 2003, and 2004; the Good Design Award in 2003; and the Urban Design Award in 2004. His works have been featured in numerous international and local publications such as *Abstract Magazine*, *xx small house*, *LE*, *hinge*, *Shotenkenchiku*, and *Shinkenchiku*.

Takaharu & Yui Tezuka

Office **Tezuka Architects, 1-19-9-3F Todoroki, Setagaya-ku, Tokyo 158-0082**

Phone/fax **+81 3 3703 7056/+81 3 3703 7038**

E-mail **tez@sepia.ocn.ne.jp**

Url **www.tezuka-arch.com**

Selected projects

1996 Soejima Hospital (Otakara, Saga Prefecture)

1999 Wood Deck House (Kamakura, Kanagawa Prefecture), Kawagoe Music House (Kawagoe, Saitama Prefecture)

2000 Machiya House (Hachioji, Tokyo), Megaphone House (Kamakura, Kanagawa Prefecture)

2001 Roof House (Hadano, Kanagawa Prefecture), Wall-less House (Setagaya-ku, Tokyo), House to Catch the Sky (Kawasaki, Kanagawa Prefecture)

2002 Saw Roof House (Ota-ku, Tokyo), Canopy House (Chofu, Tokyo)

2003 Thin Wall Office HQ#01 (Shibuya-ku, Tokyo), Toyota L&F Hiroshima (Hiroshima, Hiroshima Prefecture), Matsunoyama Natural Science Museum (Niigata Prefecture)

2004 House to Catch the Forest (Chino, Nagano), Observatory House (Kamakura, Kanagawa Prefecture)

Takaharu Tezuka was born in Tokyo in 1964. He received his MA from the University of Pennsylvania in 1990. He worked for Richard Rogers Partnership from 1990 to 1994 before returning to Japan to establish Tezuka Architects. He is currently an associate professor at Musashi Institute of Technology. Yui Tezuka was born in Kanagawa in 1969 and received her BA from Musashi Institute of Technology in 1992. She attended the Bartlett School of Architecture at University College London, before becoming a partner in Tezuka Architects in 1994. She currently lectures at Toyo University and Tokai University. The architects' largest project to date, the notable Matsunoyama Natural Science Museum, is a 120-meter-long Corten steel tube designed to withstand pressures of up to 1000 kg/m². The design enables visitors to experience and observe the changing colors of light under graduated depths of snow, the deepest point being four meters above the ground. Tezuka Architects have received numerous awards, including the Selection for the SD Review for Soejima Hospital in 1995; the Gold Prize for the Good Design Award (Japan Industrial Design Promotion Organization) for Soejima Hospital in 1997; the SD Award for Light Gauge Steel House in 1998; the Annual Architectural Commendations for Soejima Hospital in 1998; First Prize in the Matsunoyama Natural Science Museum Competition in 2001; the 18th Yoshioka Award and the JIA (Japan Institute of Architects) Best Young Architect Award for Roof House in 2002.

Hisanobu Tsujimura

Office **Hisanobu Tsujimura Design Office & Moon Balance, 378 Kameya-cho, Goko-machi Oike-agaru, Nakagyo-ku, Kyoto 604-0941**

Phone/fax **+81 75 221 6403/+81 75 221 6430**

E-mail **info@tsujimura-hisanobu.com**

Url **www.tsujimura-hisanobu.com**

Selected projects

1994 Setsugekka (Nakagyo-ku, Kyoto)

1997 Cha Cha (Naka-ku, Hiroshima), Kiss of Luminescence (Naka-ku, Hiroshima)

1998 Cha Cha 2 Moon (Naka-ku, Hiroshima)

2000 Cha Cha (Minato-ku, Tokyo), Yen (Paris, France)

2001 Cha Cha Hana (Shinjuku-ku, Tokyo), W Residence (Sakyo-ku, Kyoto)

2002 Others To Colors + TEA (Oritate, Gifu), Daishiji Temple (Mino, Osaka)

2003 Kiton (Minato-ku, Tokyo), Changes United Arrows (Naka-ku, Nagoya)

2004   Lucie (Shibuya-ku, Tokyo), Maimon (Kita-
       ku, Osaka)
2005   Sora Togetsuso Kinryu (Izu, Shizuoka
       Prefecture)

Hisanobu Tsujimura was born in Kyoto in 1961.
He set up his own studio in 1995 after working
at Livart from 1983 to 1995, and established
his own furniture line, under the *icon* label, in
2002. He is well known for his interior designs
for retail and restaurant establishments.
He currently lectures at Kyoto Prefectural
University and Kyoto Seika University. In his
projects, Tsujimura tries to create a controlled
environment by reducing the number of design
elements to the absolute minimum. He believes
that if a concept is strong and well executed,
such spaces can be changed over time without
diluting the concept, especially if the user
has an understanding and appreciation of
the essential parameters of the design intent.
His current projects include Okabe Day-Care
Condominium for the elderly, scheduled to
open in 2007, and the renovation of the service
facilities at Kyoto Station. He has received
many awards, including the Grand Prix Nashop
Lighting Contest; the Second Prize JCD (Japan
Commercial Design) Award in 1997, 1998,
1999 and 2002; and the Professional Award
for the 4th International Design Resource
Award in 2001. Also recognized for his furniture
design, Tsujimura has been regularly exhibiting
his prototype furniture at "Wa-Qu Exhibition–
Japanese Creation" in Milan since 2002 and
during Designer's Week since 2000. He
showcased his work at Tokyo Designer's Block
in 2001. He is an active member of SOU·SOU,
a designers' group producing modern designs
based on Japanese traditions.

Tomoyuki Utsumi

Office   Milligram Studio, 4-2-17 Kugahara, Ota-
         ku, Tokyo, 146-0085
Phone/fax   +81 3 5700 8155/+81 3 5700 8156
E-mail   info@milligram.ne.jp
Url   www.milligram.ne.jp

Selected projects
2000   House in Nakaikegami (Ota-ku,Tokyo)
2001   House in Sakuragawa (Itabashi-ku, Tokyo),
       Inner Skin House (Shibuya-ku,Tokyo)
2002   Nooks (Saitama, Saitama Prefecture),
       House in Senzoku (Meguro-ku, Tokyo),
       House in Hiroo (Minato-ku, Tokyo), Studio
       Flat & Passage (Minato-ku, Tokyo)
2003   House in Furuichiba (Kawasaki, Kanagawa
       Prefecture), Assortment House (Minato-
       ku, Tokyo), Skip Flat (Minato-ku, Tokyo),
       Dental Clinic at Ueki (Kamakura, Kanagawa
       Prefecture)
2004   Towered Flats (Kita-ku, Tokyo), Forest of
       Steel (Nakano-ku, Tokyo), Tavola (Saitama,
       Saitama Prefecture), White Ribbing
       (Meguro-ku, Tokyo)

Tomoyuki Utsumi was born in Mito in 1963.
He graduated from the Royal College of
Arts in London and in 1991 received his MA
from Tsukuba University. After working in the
architectural design division of Taisei Corporation
from 1992 to 1997, he established his own
practice under the name Milligram Studio, in
1998. The focus of Utsumi's work is single-family
housing, retail outlets, apartment buildings,
clinics, and offices. His conceptual work and
temporary installations include a collapsible

cottage using the "membrane system," whose
framework allows the entire cottage to fold into
a flat surface that can be stored underground
when not in use. He has also designed a spiral
wood-framed tent in London. Utsumi has been
the recipient of numerous awards, including the
AJ/Bovis Award for Architecture for the
Royal Academy Summer Exhibition in 1992.
He was also the winner of the Membrane
Structure Design Competition, sponsored by
Shinkenchiku-sha and Taiyokogyo, in 1993;
the Architecture and Environment Design
Competition, sponsored by Tokyo Gas, in
1994; and the Tokyo Society of Architects &
Building Engineers Award in 2002. His work
has been widely published in international and
local publications such as *Tokyo Houses*, *Detail*,
Jutaku Kenchiku, *Shinkenchiku*, *Casa Brutus*,
Pen, and *Esquire Japan*.

Makoto Shin Watanabe & Yoko Kinoshita

Office   ADH Architects, 3-7-18 Kaigan, Minato-
         ku, Tokyo 108-0022
Phone/fax   +81 3 3798 5561/+813 3798 5563
E-mail   adh@zag.att.ne.jp
Url   home.att.ne.jp./kiwi/adh

Selected projects
1999   NT (Chiba Prefecture)
2000   SZ (Sakura, Chiba Prefecture), TN (Tokyo)
2001   TO (Tokyo), NN (Ibaraki Prefecture)
2002   HK (Kamigori, Hyogo Prefecture), SN
       (Nagano Prefecture), NY (Kanagawa
       Prefecture)
2003   SS (Shiroishi, Miyagi Prefecture), QF
       (Doha, Quatar), KK (Tokyo)
2004   EA (Tokyo), ML (Kanagawa Prefecture),
       MC (Chiba Prefecture)

Makoto Shin Watanabe was born in Maebashi in
1950 and received his MA from Kyoto University.
He did post-graduate work at the Graduate
School of Design at Harvard University in 1979.
Watanabe worked for Arata Isozaki & Associates
from 1981 to 1987. He is currently a professor
at Hosei University. Yoko Kinoshita was born
in Tokyo in 1956 and graduated from Stanford
University. After receiving her MA from Harvard
University in 1980, she worked for Shozo Uchii &
Associates until 1987. Watanabe and Kinoshita
established ADH Architects in 1987. Kinoshita
served as a jurist at the AA School in London in
1993 and currently lectures at Nihon University,
the University of Tokyo, and Tokyo University
of Science. Watanabe and Kinoshita are also
visiting associate professors at the School of
Architecture at Washington University in St.
Louis. ADH Architects have been developing
the concept of CPS (Common spaces,
Passages or transient spaces, and Satellites
or private spaces) for homes for "non-nuclear"
families. Watanabe and Kinoshita have received
numerous awards, among them the JIA (Japan
Institute of Architects) Best Young Architect
Award in 2000; First Prize for the Shiroishi Elderly
Housing Competition in 2002; and the Best
Energy Conservation Award from the Ministry of
Economy, Trade and Industry in 2003.

Masashi & Konomi Yagi

Office   Yagi Architectural Design, 5-9-14 Hisagi
         Zushi, Kanagawa Prefecture 249-0001
Phone/fax   +81 46 870 6604/+81 46 870 6605
E-mail   yagi@zj9.so-net.ne.jp/www.yagi-arc.com

Masashi Yagi, born in Kanagawa Prefecture in
1968, received his MA from Shibaura Institute of
Technology in 1993. On graduation, he worked
for Arata Isozaki & Associates until 1999 when
he established his own practice. Konomi Yagi
was born in 1968 in Tokyo and received her MA
from Shibaura Institute of Technology in 1995.
She worked for Ogitsu Architects Studio from
2000 to 2001 before becoming an associate
principle of Yagi Architectural Design. The
house featured in this volume is the very first
project for this studio. The design philosophy of
both architects is to explore and articulate the
subtle nuances of the client's lifestyle, values,
and sensibilities into a tangible architectural
form. They refer to these nuances as the
"fourth-dimensional flow." In the house featured
in this book, the architects have skillfully used
the scenic view of the forest as an integral part
of the house by glazing the entire west side of
the building. The personality of the owner has
also been very well reflected in the house, while
the exterior has been carefully designed to
complement the house's surroundings.

Makoto Yamaguchi

Office   Makoto Yamaguchi Design Inc., 2-8-17-1F
         Minami-azabu, Minato-ku, Tokyo 106-0047
Phone/fax   +81 3 6436 0371/+81 3 6436 0372
E-mail   mail@ymgci.net
Url   www.ymgci.net

Selected projects
2000   Villa in Nakayama (Yokohama, Kanagawa
       Prefecture)
2001   Ghost—chair,(produced by WATERSTUDIO,
       manufactured by Arflex Japan)
2004   House in Shinsen (Shibuya-ku, Tokyo),
       0.6km—side table (produced by ribbon
       project)
2005   Apartment in Ebisu (Shibuya-ku, Tokyo),
       House in Todoroki (Setagaya-ku, Tokyo)

Makoto Yamaguchi was born in Chiba
Prefecture in 1972. After graduating from
Aoyamagakuin University in 1994 with an
economics degree, he decided to pursue a
career in architecture and studied at the Tokyo
National University of Fine Arts and Music.
Upon receiving his MA in 2001, Yamaguchi
established his own studio under the name
Office of Makoto Yamaguchi. Although his
designs are quite dramatic, Yamaguchi claims
that his aim is not to shock. His intention is
to thoroughly interpret and address specific
requests from each client and to provide a
unique solution to each site and situation.
Yamaguchi readily admits that people other
than the client may consider his designs
strange or inconvenient. His work has been
awarded the special prize for the INTER INTRA
SPACE Design Selection in 2001. He was
also selected as one of five finalists for the
JIA (Japan Institute of Architects) Award Best
Young Architect in 2001. Other awards he
has received include the Highly Commended
ar+d awards (The Architectural Review, UK) in
2003 and the Best Residential Project Design
Awards (Wallpaper, UK) in 2004. International
publications featuring his work include *Spazi
minimi*, *casa D*, *SPACE*, *Japanese Design
Solutions for Compact Living*, *Abitare*,
Wallpaper and *The Architectural Review*. He
lectures at Kyoto University of Art and Design
and the Shibaura Institute of Technology.

Published by Tuttle Publishing, an
imprint of Periplus Editions (HK) Ltd.

www.tuttlepublishing.com

Text © 2010 Periplus Editions (HK) Ltd
Photographs © Nacása & Partners Inc.

ISBN 978-4-8053-1126-4 hc
(previously published isbn
978-0-8048-3696-8)

Distributed by
**North America, Latin America &
Europe**
Tuttle Publishing
364 Innovation Drive
North Clarendon, VT 05759-9436
U.S.A.
Tel: 1 (802) 773-8930
Fax: 1 (802) 773-6993
info@tuttlepublishing.com
www.tuttlepublishing.com

Japan
Tuttle Publishing
Yaekari Building, 3rd Floor
5-4-12 Osaki
Shinagawa-ku
Tokyo 141 0032
Tel: (81) 3 5437-0171
Fax: (81) 3 5437-0755
sales@tuttle.co.jp
www.tuttle.co.jp

Asia Pacific
Berkeley Books Pte. Ltd.
61 Tai Seng Avenue, #02-12
Singapore 534167
Tel: (65) 6280-1330
Fax: (65) 6280-6290
inquiries@periplus.com.sg
www.periplus.com

14 13 12 11
6 5 4 3 2 1

Printed in Singapore

Endpapers: H House (page 68).
Page 1: I House (page 142).
Page 2-3: I House (page 142).
Pages 4–5: Engawa House (page 52).